TOWARDS
A NEW PHILOSOPHY
OF MANAGEMENT

The Company Development Programme of Shell UK Limited

Paul Hill

First published in Britain by Gower Press Limited
140 Great Portland Street, London W1N 5TA
1971

Set in 11 on 13 point Times and printed in Britain by
Tonbridge Printers Ltd
Peach Hall Works, Tonbridge, Kent

Contents

Part Five

EFFECT ON PRODUCTIVITY BARGAINING

Part Six

CONCLUSIONS

EPILOGUE

Illustrations

Foreword

It has frequently been said that the troubles of the modern world are due to a fantastically rapid rate of technological advance coupled with relatively slow social progress. The difficulties of making social changes are certainly well illustrated in this book, which describes an attempt by the sophisticated management of part of a large science-based industry, helped by a leading group of practising social scientists, to modify the organisation and the norms of the teams responsible for the operation and maintenance of several of their oil refineries.

The Shell companies have a world-wide reputation for their scientific research and the skilled application of science to all aspects of their technological enterprise. They have been among the earliest encouragers of enlightened education for scientists and engineers. They have supported the great post-war developments in education in management. It is not surprising, therefore, that when one of these companies, Shell UK Ltd (formerly Shell Refining Co Ltd), became concerned about the poor industrial relations, low morale and productivity per man in their plants, particularly when compared with performance in similar plants in the US, efforts were made to examine and better the organisation. What is interesting is that they invited the co-operation of the Tavistock Institute of Human Relations, a group of social scientists not at all wedded to the ideas of scientific management with its apparatus of work study, job evaluation, organisational charts and its focus on machine-oriented tasks. This group had developed, as a result of the pioneering work of Eric L Trist, the concept that the social organisation for a given task was at least as important as the arrangement of the technical equipment, that men were not here merely to mind machines, but that machines were an extension of the minds and fingers of the men who had responsibility for the task.

E L Trist (1951) and A K Rice (1958) had shown that this social approach could lead to a restructuring of manufacturing groups which produced better output and improved morale. The system whose performance needs to be optimised does not therefore consist only of the process plant and its control equipment, but includes the human beings in their various roles as managers, operators and craftsmen. The Shell employee relations planning unit and the Tavistock Institute team accepted that the problem was to optimise the socio-technical system, and set out to persuade the organisation of the importance of defining their objectives in these terms and of finding ways to implement them.

The story is told this time not by a member of the Tavistock team, but by Charles Paul Hill, an employee of Shell UK Ltd appointed to lead their employee relations planning unit during the first two years of the project, which included the period of diagnosis and initiation and the start of implementation. Subsequently as a member of the Group personnel department in Shell International Petroleum Company he was able to keep in touch with the programme from a more objective viewpoint.

Mr Hill's account is balanced and straightforward. It will appeal to all interested in social organisation, to managers, sociologists, trade unionists, and especially to fellow workers in personnel and staff management, whose aspirations are tempered by the harsh realities of British industry, the world's oldest industrial society. It is a case history of a substantial effort in management which resulted in a substantial but qualified success. It shows how much more attention needs to be directed to the problems of motivation and satisfaction in the industrial society in which we shall have to live our lives and earn our living.

Sir Winston Churchill founded Churchill College at Cambridge as his national memorial because he saw the need for encouraging education and research in applied science and technology in a university atmosphere. With the help of its Industrial Advisers the College has been able to offer Industrial Fellow Commonerships to selected workers in fields of relevance to the technological environment on which our national livelihood depends. We are grateful to the Shell Group for introducing Paul Hill to the College and happy to have been able to give him the opportunity as an Industrial Fellow Commoner to record this personal account of an important experiment in management.

W R Hawthorne
Churchill College, Cambridge

Preface

This book describes a long-term development programme which Shell UK Limited embarked upon in 1965, with assistance from the Tavistock Institute's Human Resources Centre. The aim of the programme was to improve company performance through creating conditions in which people at all levels could become more highly motivated and more committed to their tasks.

As the leader of the company's employee relations planning team (ERP), which proposed the programme and helped to carry it through, I was in a privileged position to observe and take part in its initial growth across the company. In late 1967 I moved to a London-based role in Shell International Petroleum Company, and although no longer directly involved in the Shell UK Limited programme, I was able to keep in touch with developments there. I have tried to give an objective picture of the complex process of change which emerged, the successes achieved so far, and the set-backs and disappointments.

The account represents my personal interpretation of the programme, not that of the company. That I have been able to write it is due to the opportunity afforded me by Shell International Petroleum Company to take up an appointment as Industrial Fellow Commoner at Churchill College, Cambridge, for a year; and to the freedom granted me by Shell UK Limited to write about the programme as I saw it. I am grateful to the management of both companies, and to the Master and Fellows of Churchill for a sympathetic and supportive atmosphere in which to write.

Whilst accepting full responsibility for its contents, I am grateful to the many other people who have helped me, directly or indirectly, with the writing of this book: numerous colleagues at many levels in Shell UK Limited, regrettably too many to name; the other members of the ERP team—David O'Brien, Michael Clark, Bill Woollard and Geoff Hibbert; the members of the Tavistock Human Resources Centre, (all named in the text), particularly Eric Trist and Fred Emery who were heavily involved in the first two years of the programme, and Michael Foster who became the main collaborater thereafter. Especially profitable was the opportunity to spend two weeks with Eric Trist at the University of Pennsylvania's Management and Behavioural Sciences Center, to get his valuable comments on the manuscript, and complete my final revision there.

Paul Hill

Part One
BACKGROUND
TO THE EXPERIMENT

Chapter 1

The Motivation Problem in Industry

The problem of how people become motivated to work effectively in organisations is not a new one. It has been concerning managers of organisations in industrialised societies for many years. But there is evidence which suggests that in spite of awareness and concern about the problem it is still growing. It is difficult to know how to measure the scale of the problem, but one indication is the extent to which work people take part in stoppages which involve the loss of working days.

In the United Kingdom, statistics published by the Department of Employment show that the number of stoppages occurring and the amount of time lost through strike action are currently following an alarming upward trend. As can be seen from Figure 1:1 the number of stoppages in all UK industries and services has been going up each year since 1966. The total of 3116 stoppages in 1969 was a record since statistics have been kept and a new peak of 3886 was reached in 1970. Figure 1:2 shows a similarly unfavourable trend in the number of working days lost as the result of work stoppages. The figures do not include time lost as the result of "political" strike action, nor do they include time lost by people who were laid off as the result of stoppages at establishments other than where they took place. The 1969 total was the highest recorded since the general strike in 1926 and the total for 1970 far exceeded that of 1969. It does not seem likely that 1971 will show much improvement.

The number of working days lost in any one year can be influenced by exceptionally large stoppages. When, however, the loss of working

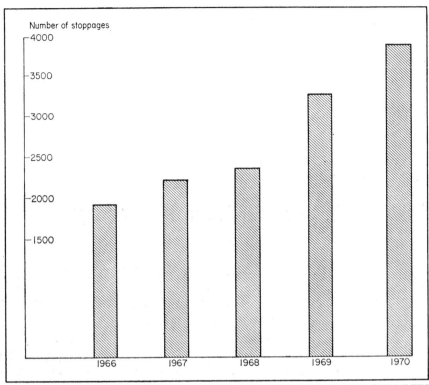

FIGURE 1:1   UK WORK STOPPAGES IN ALL INDUSTRIES AND SERVICES
1966–70
(*Employment and Productivity Gazette*)

days and the number of stoppages occurring are considered together, it
is clear that the trend in the UK over the last five years is a highly
adverse one and that the massive increase in working days lost in 1969
and 1970 is not simply due to a few very large-scale or lengthy stoppages.
The general picture is a positive trend towards more stoppages and more
time lost.

The reasons for this unfavourable trend are not easy to specify. The
biggest single contributory factor is an increase in the percentage of
strikes over the period 1966 to 1970 which are related to the issue of
wages. Whilst the wages issue is clearly of growing importance, it would
be a mistake to explain the adverse trend of the statistics purely in
economic terms or purely in terms of inadequate bargaining machinery.
Many wage-related strikes tend to be of long duration and to involve
large numbers of employees. A large percentage of the total stoppages,
however, are relatively small-scale affairs and of short duration. In

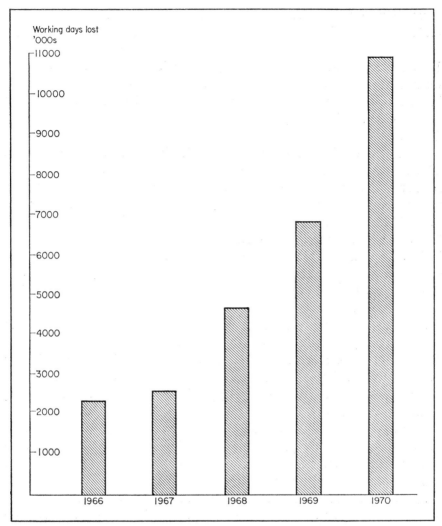

FIGURE 1:2 UK WORKING DAYS LOST IN ALL INDUSTRIES AND
SERVICES 1966-70
(*Employment and Productivity Gazette*)

1969, for example, according to the *Employment and Productivity Gazette,* nearly 50 per cent of all strikes lasted not more than two days, 44 per cent involved less than 100 workers and 63 per cent resulted in the loss of less than 500 working days.

It must be assumed, therefore, that underlying the greater willingness of people to go on strike about wage-related matters is a more widespread deterioration in their attitudes towards their work, a growing sense of unrest and discontent and a diminishing level of commitment and motivation. This assumption is supported by a number of arguments:

1   The wages issue is a useful peg on which to hang a strike. It is likely that many stoppages called in support of a wage demand are also in part a reaction to other forms of grievance which, without the wages peg, would have found expression in other ways.

2   The stoppages which actually take place are often only the visible portion of the iceberg. Hidden from public view is the massive platform of restrictive practices and inefficiency which lead to a serious and regular loss of productive effort. The likelihood is that an increase in the number of strikes taking place represents a corresponding widening of the hidden platform.

3   A large majority of strikes are unofficial. The Donovan Commission in 1968 reported that during the period 1964–6 as many as 95 per cent of all strikes were unofficial. If this percentage applies equally to strikes called in 1969 and 1970 this would be consistent with a state of widespread discontent among work people and a growing willingness to disrupt an organisation's activities through unofficial strikes without first exhausting agreed negotiating procedures.

4   Wider sectors of society are becoming involved in strike action or the threat of it. Large firms like Vauxhall or Pilkington, which once seemed to be immune to the general problem of labour disputes owing to the trouble they took over joint consultation and to their image as good employers, have now been shown to be as vulnerable as the rest. Professional work people—doctors, teachers, nurses—groups whose loyalty and commitment to their vocation once made the idea of a withdrawal of the services they render to society unthinkable, now contemplate or take such action almost as a matter of course.

5   A growing number of people in staff grades of employment are becoming unionised. This indicates that an increasing number of people in administrative or supervisory roles are no longer satisfied to have their relationships with their employer regulated on the basis of an individual contract. There appears to be a growing need for some form of outside representation to deal with managements on their behalf or perhaps, in some cases, to protect them.

In summary, therefore, the picture that emerges demonstrates that an increasing number and a widening range of people in the UK are expressing discontent with some aspects of their jobs; or to put it in other terms, the problem of motivating people in organisations to work effectively and conscientiously is a growing one.

WHY THE PROBLEM IS GROWING

The obvious reason for the growth of the problem outlined above is that more people are becoming concerned about their wages and are apparently now more willing than in past years to take strike action to secure a bigger share of the cake. This aspect of the problem is clearly of great importance and has led to wide recognition of the need to improve methods and procedures of wage bargaining through persuasion and legislation.

There are, however, perhaps less-obvious reasons which can be advanced to explain the growth of the motivation problem in recent years.

People's expectations

For example, the level of people's expectations is rising. The benefits which a highly developed society offers its members—a better level of education and a more responsible social status—serve at the same time to increase the level of their expectations. As this process continues, well-educated work people are unlikely to be content with jobs which in no way match up to what they have learnt to expect. Confronted with boring jobs for which they can feel no enthusiasm, their frustration may well express itself in strike action or in some more moderate form of revolt against the system such as going slow or working to rule.

Changing values

The emerging values of industrialised society seem to be changing in the same direction. There is a growing recognition of the need for individuals to achieve self-expression and self-fulfilment in the sense of realising their capabilities. There is, therefore, a general challenge to society which goes beyond the traditional "young Turks" phenomenon. Whereas the "young Turks" have always been anxious to take over the leadership of the system, the current stress is on challenging and changing the system itself. Up till the present it is the academic world which has been the main target for change and which has provided in the wave of student revolt an obvious, if extreme, manifestation of the effect of changing values. These same needs for self-fulfilment have implications also for industrial organisations and it would not be surprising if the same spirit of challenge and revolt evident in the academic world were now beginning to contribute to the worsening problem of motivation in organisations. There are already signs of this in the United States.

Organisational changes

Many large organisations have themselves made changes in recent years which tend to aggravate the problem of motivation. Faced with the need to cut costs in a hard and competitive economic climate, they have abandoned their traditional role of paternalistic provider to their employees. Whilst the paternal role would not have been in tune with the needs of the young generation of work people, it had in past years undoubtedly stimulated a feeling of loyalty and dedication to the organisation in many older employees. Now it has gone and it does not seem that anything has been put in its place.

Technological change is also in some cases aggravating the problem when it creates more jobs of a dull and routine nature.

More extreme in their effects have been the numerous mergers of recent years. Whilst no doubt justified on economic and rational grounds, they have in some cases demonstrated very clearly to work people that jobs that once seemed completely secure are no longer so and that the old notion of loyalty to and identification with an organisation is out of date. Along with it has disappeared, it would seem, the old value of "a fair day's work for a fair day's pay."

Mass media

In their wide and detailed coverage of events which have to do with change or revolt—demonstrations, strikes, sit-ins or riots—the mass media are undoubtedly hastening the process of change. The effect is to intensify awareness of the problems which organisations face regarding work motivation, without contributing to their solution.

EFFORTS TO DEAL WITH THE MOTIVATION PROBLEM

Whilst it is doubtful if the rate at which the motivation problem is likely to grow is widely appreciated, the existence of the problem is well recognised and much has already been done in response to it. Some of these responses are reviewed in the remainder of this chapter.

The leisure theory

One response which may have certain superficial attraction is to argue that there is no real need to attempt to solve the problem of motivating people at work since before too long the effects of technological advance and increasing automation will be to expand enormously people's leisure time and to reduce to a minimum the amount of time they will have to spend at work.

Such notions have derived from the work of social scientists like Herman Kahn (1967) who have attempted to predict the likely shape of society in the future. Kahn suggests that by the end of this century the normal basic working week in the US may have been reduced from the current forty hours to an average of thirty hours or even less.

Leaving aside the question of how people in that situation would handle their increased leisure time, there is little evidence that the actual length of the working week is likely to decrease significantly within the next decade at least outside the United States, where the four-day week has begun to make an appearance. Experience in the UK has been that although the number of formal working hours in the week has been slowly but progressively reduced since the Second World War from a norm of about forty-seven hours to a current norm of forty hours, the actual number of hours, including overtime, spent at work by people in manufacturing industry has tended to decline only slightly. For example, official figures indicate that in manufacturing industry during 1969, the average number of hours worked in the week was still close to forty-five.

Joint consultation

Since the war various systems of joint consultation which allow worker representation on high level works councils or even on the boards of organisations have been developed in several countries in Europe: for example, in Jugoslavia, Germany, France, Holland and in the nationalised industries in Britain.

Proponents of these systems would argue that the involvement of employee representatives in major works councils' activities or in the decision-making process of the board should have the effect of ensuring that the viewpoint of the employees is considered before decisions are made and of helping accordingly to reduce organisational conflict. In theory this should lead to a better climate, higher morale and improved performance. Various studies of some of these systems have been made but there seems to be no evidence that they have any impact on the level of the individual worker's commitment to his job nor on his motivation to carry it out effectively (Emery and Thorsrud 1964, 1969). The picture is rather that the average employee tends to be relatively unaware of how the joint consultation system functions in his organisation. Influence exerted by the employee representatives tends to be limited to the welfare or "personnel" aspects of the job.

Whatever other benefits such systems of employee representation may confer therefore they would certainly not seem likely on present evidence to contribute to the solution of the motivational problem as it has been described in the earlier part of this chapter.

Participation
The most promising approach to dealing with the problem of motivation has been the work and research carried out by social scientists since the Second World War in the field of direct participation: that is, the greater involvement of the individual in decisions which affect the way he plans and carries out his own job. This work, the attempt to improve organisational performance through the more effective use of people which is now normally referred to as "organisation development," has grown up on both sides of the Atlantic but with the major effort centred in the United States. That the US should have devoted the most effort to dealing with the motivation problem is due not only to their greater resources and their highly developed system of consultancy linkages between the academic world and industry but also to the fact that the changes in society and in the industrial environment, which have largely caused the problem, were occurring earlier and faster in the US than anywhere else in the world.

Nevertheless, the work in Europe, although conducted on a smaller scale and with a different emphasis, was leading to similar conclusions. It has from the beginning paid much more attention to the shop floor than the American work, which has been rather exclusively concerned with management. Much of the conceptualisation and development of theory in this area in the UK has been carried out by the Tavistock Institute of Human Relations. As the Institute was to be the outside research organisation involved in Shell UK Limited's development programme, their work is described in Chapter 3 and need not be included here.

The general conclusions reached by many different social scientists are matched by the experience of a growing number of managers—that the traditional bureaucratically structured organisation, with its authority concentrated at the top of the hierarchy, seems no longer an appropriate or effective means of coping with the rapidly changing environment in which organisations now have to operate. What seems to be needed is a more flexible organisational structure, new management values concerning the use of people, a more participative climate and new ways of involving people down the line in decision-making.

SOME ORGANISATION DEVELOPMENT APPROACHES

Whilst theoretical conclusions on both sides of the Atlantic have much in common, there has been a significant difference in emphasis between the US and the UK in the way in which attempts have been made to put the theories into practice. In the US, the main post-war thrust towards producing change in organisations sprang from the work of Kurt Lewin (1952) and his studies in group attitudes and behaviour, which led to the development of T-groups and to the foundation of the National Training Laboratory (NTL).

In the UK, efforts have in general concentrated more on analysis of the organisation structure as a starting point than on the area of interpersonal relationships as in the US. A further general distinction is that, whereas in the US some form of training experience has often served as the entry point to organisation development, in the UK the tendency has been to initiate an organisational change process and then to follow this with such training as has been shown to be necessary. An example of this was the change programme developed by the Glacier Metal Company (described in Chapter 3), which was later followed by the establishment of the Glacier Institute of Management, which gave training courses to members of the company and to people from outside.

No attempt is made below to carry out a comprehensive review of the various methods and techniques of organisation development but examples are given of some salient approaches which are currently available to managers of organisations.

T-groups
The idea of the T-group—which stands for training-group—was that by bringing a group of strangers together in a so-called "laboratory" situation, away from their normal environment, and by allowing them to interact, without any agenda or programme of work over a period of time, they would all learn a lot about their behaviour in groups and gain valuable insights about their own strengths and weaknesses which they could not get in any other way.

This process of learning, which has also been called sensitivity training, or group dynamics, has shown that most groups, put into the laboratory situation, will follow a predictable pattern of development. The first stage has been termed "unfreezing." The members sound each other out and in the absence of a formal agenda and the usual props of status or role, the normal conventions which inhibit frankness and openness are broken down, or unfrozen. In the second stage, the members are open to new learning, about how they affect other people, and how they react to others. They are free to experiment with new ways of behaving and to receive, perhaps for the first time in their lives, honest feedback from the group. The final stage is refreezing, during which hopefully the members build into themselves what they have learned and the group typically ends up with a feeling of great solidarity and mutual warmth and support.

The unfreezing and learning parts of the process are uncomfortable for many people and can be very painful for some. It is therefore essential that the group should be guided, when necessary, by an experienced trainer.

Impressed by the original work of the stranger laboratories, a number of organisations in the US set up internal T-group programmes for their own staff. This led to the development of new groups, known as cousin laboratories or family laboratories, where the members were organisationally related, either diagonally across departments, or vertically within a department. Such groupings clearly imposed additional stresses, since the members would continue to work together after their T-group experience and would not go off on their separate ways. It was hoped, however, that the new forms of laboratory training would make the learning more relevant to the members' performance in the organisation.

The T-group in its various forms is still used by many corporations in the US and Canada. Whilst it can undoubtedly provide valuable experience and learning for some individuals, there seems to be no evidence that it can, on its own, improve organisational performance. Many organisations, in fact, now use the T-group merely as an introduction to a wider programme of organisation development, claiming that it helps to solve inter-personal problems and create a more open climate in which change can subsequently take place.

In the UK and in Europe there has been very much less emphasis on the T-group than in the US. It is possible to attend a sensitivity training laboratory in the UK and the European counterpart of NTL, the European Institute for Transnational studies in group and organisation development (EIT) was established in 1962. However, large-scale programmes of T-groups within organisations on the American pattern of the sixties have not been attempted. Moreover there are signs in the US of less emphasis being placed on a merely inter-personal approach.

The training package
An important derivative of the T-group has been the training package. These are package programmes of varying levels of sophistication which set out to help managements improve the performance of their organisations through following carefully phased stages. The programme usually includes facilities for training some of the internal people from the organisation in the techniques of the approach so that they can play the role of internal consultants and take over from the original marketers of the programme. A feature of the package approach to organisation development, which is often attractive to managements, is that they seem to present a clear and logical path to organisational improvement whereas other less structured approaches may appear somewhat vague and risky by comparison. The best known package is the Managerial Grid programme (Blake 1964). This is a sophisticated six-phase programme, which incorporates certain features of the T-group, but is geared more closely to organisational improvement.

The basic concept is that a manager's behaviour can be plotted on a two-dimensional grid, which indicates the degree of concern for people and concern for production implicit in his actions. It is argued that the optimum style in normal situations would be where a manager demonstrates maximum concern both for production and for the people involved in his actions.

Phase I of the programme is a one-week educational seminar, prior to which members are asked to do about forty hours' preparatory work. Through exercises and case studies, teams of managers learn to use the grid and to analyse their own and others' behaviour. They also attempt an analysis of the prevailing management style of their own organisation. Towards the end of the week, each manager is told by the rest of his team where they would place his behaviour on the grid.

Subsequent phases are designed to: II improve actual team performance, III help solve inter-group problems, IV assist with the production of short- and long-term objectives to improve organisational performance and V involve managers in plans to achieve these objectives.

The final phase, VI, is for review and evaluation of what has been achieved.

The whole six-phase programme would probably last for four years or more. In practice, however, many organisations tend to stop after phase I and it is difficult so far to find objective accounts of the overall programme's effectiveness.

Examples of other package approaches are Bill Reddin's three-dimensional programme, which has many similarities with the Blake Managerial Grid; a three-phase programme devised by the Netherlands Pedagogic Institute, and a recent "Organisation Renewal" programme produced by Gordon Lippitt (1969).

Another programme being used by some companies in the UK is the one devised by Ralph Coverdale. Although his method is far less structured than Blake's, it starts off with a week's seminar at which groups of managers learn, by process of trial and error, how they can work more effectively as a team. Coverdale also utilises the training of internal people from the organisation to help spread the learning down the line.

Job enrichment

An important method of seeking improved performance of people in discrete parts of organisations is the technique of job enrichment developed by Frederick Herzberg. This is not linked with T-groups. It is based on a theory of motivation derived from research into the factors which cause job satisfaction or dissatisfaction in the work situation (Herzberg, 1959).

Basically his theory is that quite different sets of factors are responsible for people feeling satisfied or dissatisfied at work. Those which cause dissatisfaction he calls hygiene factors. These are things which form the work environment, but are not part of the job itself: for example, working conditions, company policy and regulations, salary, job security, etc. If these factors are not adequately looked after people get dissatisfied. But once they are adequate, making them better will not cause positive satisfaction.

The factors which can cause positive satisfaction, he calls motivators. These are things which derive from the actual jobs that people do: for example, responsibility, achievement, recognition and growth. Improvement in motivation can come from building into their jobs the opportunity for people to experience these motivators: in other words, from enriching their jobs. In applying this technique within organisations,

Herzberg selected a group whose jobs would be enriched and a similar group where no changes would be made and which would therefore serve as a control. To prevent any "Hawthorne effect" among the experimental group (that is, to prevent any change in their performance, simply because they know they were the subject of a special study), discussion of how to enrich their jobs was carried out with managers not closer than two levels above the group itself. Changes would then be gradually introduced and the group's performance compared with that of the control group.

Several studies have been reported which show a significant improvement in motivation and performance of the group whose jobs had been enriched (Ford, 1969).

Job enrichment has also been successfully tried out in the UK by one of Herzberg's previous colleagues, Bill Paul. (Paul and Robertson, 1970.) During 1969, for example, he did some work at Stanlow Refinery, the results of which are described in Chapter 16.

Survey feedback methods
A number of centres, such as the Institute of Social Research in Michigan, US (Floyd Mann, 1957) and the Ashridge Management College in the UK (Sadler, 1970), have developed methods of improving organisational performance based on gathering data about the organisation and its functioning and then feeding the data back to the organisation's managers. This action research approach has proved an effective method of highlighting weaknesses and areas where improvement of of some kind is needed. Clearly, however, it can be effective only so far as the organisation is prepared to take action on the data the survey provides.

Management by objectives
A number of approaches to organisation development on both sides of the Atlantic are focused on a system of management by objectives, a concept originally popularised by Peter Drucker in the early fifties. The best known method in the UK is probably the one described by John Humble, (Humble, 1968). Essentially the system involves the identification of the key results attaching to each role in the organisation, and the joint specification between the role holder and his manager of concrete targets to be achieved in the key results areas during the ensuing work period. Progress reviews are held and steps taken to remove any obstacles preventing achievement of the targets.

SHELL UK LIMITED'S COMPANY DEVELOPMENT PROGRAMME

Whilst there is a lot of activity and experimentation in the field of organisation development, and whilst it seems that many managements are interested in exploring the value of the sort of approaches described above, there are as yet relatively few examples of companies which have planned and put into effect a large-scale and comprehensive organisation development programme. The programme devised and implemented by Shell UK Limited, which this book will describe, is one such example.

It was a programme developed by the company, in collaboration with the Tavistock Institute, and launched in 1965. It was seen as a long-term project of five to ten years' duration. Its aims were to improve the motivation of employees at all levels and to remove unnecessary conflict from the work situation. It was expected that as a result of the programme people would become more committed to the achievement of company objectives and that productivity and profitability would accordingly be enhanced. The development programme included a number of unique features and achieved considerable success. The body of the book will give an objective account of how the programme was planned and devised, how it was put into operation and the effects it had on management and men. The concluding chapters will attempt an evaluation of the progress achieved and will consider what general implications can be drawn from Shell UK Limited's experience in this field.

First, however, it is necessary to give in Chapter 2 sufficient background information about the company to make the programme understandable; and in Chapter 3 a summary of the earlier work of the Tavistock Institute to show how this had led to the formulation of the concepts which would be built into the company development programme.

Chapter 2

Background of Shell UK Limited

Shell UK Limited, the company with which this book is concerned, is a member of the Royal Dutch/Shell Group of companies. The Royal Dutch/Shell Group is a large multi-national organisation, with its centre partly in The Hague and partly in London, and with approximately 500 operating companies located in over 100 countries throughout the free world.

The Group maintains oil and chemical service companies at the centre which provide advice and assistance to operating companies by way of contractual service arrangements. It is nevertheless a key principle that each operating company enjoys a high degree of autonomy. Certain activities can clearly be most effectively dealt with at the centre: for example, the balancing of international oil supply against demand; the co-ordination of forward planning; or career planning to produce staff required for senior international job postings. But each operating company is a separate corporate entity and its management is responsible for the effective utilisation of resources and the achievement of the company's short- and long-term objectives.

ROLE AND STRUCTURE OF SHELL UK LIMITED

Shell UK Limited is one of these largely autonomous operating companies. It should be explained that at the time the development programme was launched in 1965, the name of the company was Shell Refining Company Limited. In 1967, however, that company became part of a larger organisation, Shell UK Limited, which was responsible, in addition to oil refining, for Shell's exploration and production activities in the North Sea. For the sake of consistency, the company will be referred to throughout this account as Shell UK Limited, it being understood that this refers up to mid-1967 to Shell Refining Company Limited, and after mid-1967 to the oil manufacturing activities of the present Shell UK Limited.

The business of the company in 1965 was to meet market demands for petroleum products in the UK through the processing of crude oils or other feedstocks allocated to it by the Group's central supply unit. As a general rule, products were sold to the market through a separate company, Shell-Mex and BP Limited, so that Shell UK Limited did not have direct contact with the market, neither for the purchase of its crude oil intake, nor for the sale of its products.

The structure of the company in 1965, showing the locations involved in the development programme, is outlined in Figure 2:1. The total refining capacity at that time was approximately 21 million tons a year and the number of people employed was approximately 6460. This included some 670 employees working on the chemical plants at the two major locations, Shell Haven and Stanlow. Although they were operationally part of Shell Chemical Company Limited, they were to participate in the development programme alongside the refinery employees.

Unlike some refineries which can be designed and programmed to process a single crude oil on a long-term basis, both Shell Haven and Stanlow are known as "balancing" refineries. This means they have to be prepared to process a wide variety of differing crude oils and to deal with frequent changes in feedstock so as to help balance out the effect of programme revisions due to difficulties over supply or manufacture occurring in other parts of the world.

Both Shell Haven, near Stanford-le-Hope in Essex, and Stanlow, at Ellesmere Port in Cheshire, started as installation and storage sites some fifty years ago. Both have expanded enormously since the Second World War. Ardrossan, in Ayrshire, was a small bitumen refinery with a tradition of good relationships and a relatively stable level of operations. A further small refinery, Heysham, in Lancashire, with a refining capacity of approximately two million tons per annum, is not shown in Figure 2:1, since, due to close operational ties and shared services with an ICI plant on the adjoining site, its management decided it could not fully take part in the development programme. Finally, a major new refinery was planned for Teesside, and preparation of the site had already started in 1965. An account of the way in which Teesport

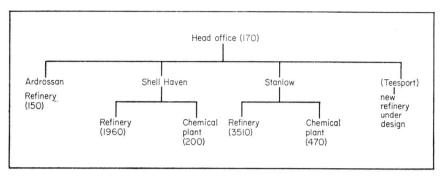

FIGURE 2:1 SHELL UK LIMITED—COMPANY ORGANISATION IN 1965
Showing locations involved in the development programme

refinery was influenced by the development programme is given in Chapter 13.

HISTORY OF MOTIVATION PROBLEM IN THE COMPANY

It is necessary to go back in history somewhat, to show that the problem of motivating people to work effectively—especially at shop-floor level —was of long standing in the company. The problem really started in the early 1950s, after the major plant expansions at Shell Haven and Stanlow. It seemed by the early 1960s still to be growing, particularly at Shell Haven. By then, the problem was threatening to assume for many people in supervisory roles an aspect of inevitability, something so deep-rooted that it appeared it could never be solved.

The difficulties were not, of course, vastly different from, nor probably any worse than, those suffered by many other companies in the UK at the time. But being aware of this did not make the situation any more palatable to the managers and the personnel people principally involved in dealing with it.

Pattern of union negotiations

A general factor which, while not a cause of the motivational problem, sometimes tended to aggravate its effects, was the complicated pattern of negotiating arrangements the company had with the unions representing the shop-floor employees.

All process operators, and other non-craft workers, were represented by the Transport and General Workers Union (TGWU). The company's agreement with the union was on a national level, so that its provisions

C

applied equally to all three refineries, and increases in the basic rate of pay, for example, were negotiated centrally through the head office.

Craftsmen were represented by their respective craft unions, of which there were, during the early 1960s, ten at Shell Haven and nine at Stanlow. (The unions involved are detailed in Appendix 1.) Negotiations were conducted at local level between the refinery management and a joint union negotiating committee formed of representatives from each of the craft unions involved. As the agreements were local, their provisions varied between refineries and increases in wage rates could be negotiated separately at each location.

Negotiation of amendments to any provisions of the union agreements was handled between management and the union officials. There were, however, at each refinery shop steward committees which played an important role in discussing the interpretation and application of the agreements. At Shell Haven and Stanlow, there were separate committees for the TGWU and the craft shop stewards respectively.

In some ways this mixture of a centralised agreement with the TGWU and local agreements with the craft unions presented the company with the worst of both worlds. On the one hand, potentially useful developments with the local TGWU branch at one refinery could sometimes not be pursued, because any changes in the agreement had to be negotiated centrally and the union could not achieve a consensus. On the other hand, costly settlements with the craft unions due to special factors at one refinery, which in theory should have been confined to that location, tended nevertheless to spread through the whole system.

The reason it spread was that at each refinery there was a traditional, though quite unofficial relationship between the rates of pay of the craftsmen and the operators. If the craftsmen's rates were increased, there were very strong pressures to re-establish the customary differential by increasing the operators' rate. Even so, had the union agreement covering operators been a local one, it should have been possible to contain the rate increases within the one location concerned. Because the TGWU agreement was a national one, however, any wage rate incease for operators automatically applied to all the refineries. The final link in the chain would therefore be claims from craftsmen at the refineries other than the one where the first increase took place, for re-establishment of their differentials *vis-à-vis* the operators.

The effect of this type of leap-frogging claim pattern was damaging to the morale of many managers and supervisors. It suggested that the unions held all the power and initiative and that the company had little control over events and no strategy of its own to pursue. It reinforced, therefore, the impression that the problem of motivating people effectively at shop-floor level was unlikely to be solved.

Some practical aspects of the motivation problem are described below in order to give the flavour of the situation in which the company development programme was to be launched. Examples are taken from Shell Haven, where the problem was considerably more acute than at Stanlow.

Demarcation disputes

Restrictions on the level of shop-floor productivity were imposed by strict demarcation lines between the crafts, and between craftsmen and process operators. This meant that a craftsman, who was perfectly capable of carrying out minor ancillary tasks connected with his own main task, was not allowed to do so if those ancillary tasks "belonged" to another craft. On the same grounds, process operators were prevented from doing simple maintenance tasks on the units, even although they had the time and the ability to do them. The result of these restrictions was that more men than were in practical terms necessary had regularly to be scheduled to work on many jobs throughout the refinery.

A further complication was that there was not always mutual agreement between the crafts about where the demarcation lines lay. A job allocated to one craft could therefore, at a strategic moment, be claimed by another. When this happened, the situation often quickly developed where each of the two crafts involved threatened to go on strike if the other carried out the work. Clearly this was a fertile field where disputes could be planted and could mushroom into extremely difficult situations for the manager who wanted the job done, but who was naturally reluctant to cause a strike of any section of the workforce.

Overtime earnings

A major factor contributing to a low level of productivity was the pattern of high overtime earnings which had grown up at the refineries, particularly on the craft side. Men came to rely on receiving these earnings and resisted strongly any changes which would result in a reduced need for overtime working. This was, of course, a very common pattern throughout UK industry. Applicants for refinery jobs would invariably ask what opportunity they would have for overtime earnings. Whilst the standard reply was that there could be no guarantee of regular overtime, in practice, many employees did expect and work regular overtime.

There were two main reasons for the establishment of this pattern in the refinery. Both combined to bring pressure on supervisors and managers to authorise high overtime levels. They were, first, the fact that overtime was voluntary; and, second, the fact that in order to complete major plant overhauls on schedule, or to deal with urgent repair jobs, overtime working was essential.

Since overtime was voluntary, a craftsman could refuse to work overtime on an urgent and important task without in any way contravening the union agreement. This gave the shop stewards great power to extract concessions about future overtime arrangements from managers who faced the alternative of shutting down costly plant.

Two specific examples of such concessions will illustrate the point. One craft had only a small number of men employed at Shell Haven, but it was essential that one of them should take part in many urgent jobs, some of which occurred at weekends, and were therefore carried out on overtime. This led, over a period of time, to the establishment of an unofficial rule: if one member of the craft was needed for weekend overtime, all his colleagues in the same craft should also be brought in for overtime. A principle of "all in, or none in."

The second example was more general in its application, but had been achieved by similar pressures brought to bear on managers at critical times. It was the rule—again unofficial—that contractors' men hired to supplement the refinery maintenance force on major overhaul work should not be allowed to work overtime, until all refinery employees in the relevant crafts had themselves first been offered overtime.

By the early 1960s, therefore, the general situation was that refinery efficiency often had to suffer as the result of the determination of some employees to defend their overtime earnings. Men would typically refuse to co-operate over the introduction of new working methods which would reduce overtime opportunities. Given the pattern of overtime earnings which had grown up, this was not at all surprising. Nevertheless, it seemed as if they, on the one hand, and managers and supervisors, on the other, were sometimes working towards completely different objectives.

Resistance to strength reductions

At Shell Haven there was strong opposition from the shop stewards to any reduction in the number of their members employed. This applied both to crafts and to operators. It was particularly difficult to achieve a reduction in the number of shift operators working on the process units, even where technical changes had clearly reduced the work load to a significant extent. Whilst in theory, the number of people employed was not a bargainable issue, it being one of management's so-called prerogatives, in practice it was highly desirable to achieve agreement to any reductions. Where changes were imposed without such agreement, a number of sanctions—such as "working to rule"—could be applied, which could have a serious effect on refinery efficiency.

The success of the resistance to reductions in numbers at Shell Haven is shown by the fact that whereas, through non-replacement of normal wastage in the four years up to 1964, a reduction in the number of hourly paid employees of about 5 per cent a year was achieved at Ardrossan and Stanlow, the comparable reduction at Shell Haven was only about 1 per cent a year.

Morale

It is not surprising that the morale of employees suffered as the result of the succession of disputes engendered by the restrictive practices described above. The people whose morale suffered most were probably the supervisors, who saw their authority being constantly eroded by concessions to the unions and to the shop stewards.

Whilst management's relationships with union officials and shop stewards were usually cordial enough at the personal level, they were under-laid with a deep mistrust and suspicion which was completely mutual. Any proposal put forward by either side would normally be carefully scrutinised by the other to discover hidden motives and implications.

Effects of these difficulties

At Shell Haven, where the situation was worst, the low level of productivity and the relatively high labour cost of running units was, by the early 1960s, adversely affecting the likelihood of future expansion there. At Stanlow, the situation was not so serious but the trend was a deteriorating one. At Ardrossan, as could be expected of a small and remote location in an area with a tradition of good relationships, there were few problems.

At the two major refineries, the personnel people and many line managers were kept fully stretched in coping with day-to-day difficulties. There was little opportunity for forward planning. At shop-floor level, and at the union bargaining level, the company seemed unable to do anything more than respond under pressure to union initiatives.

There was, therefore, a strong feeling among many managers that the company should equip itself to do some long-term forward planning in the personnel field, so that it could break away from the fire-fighting role, decide where it wanted to go and take some appropriate initiatives in its relationships with its employees and with the unions.

EMPLOYEE RELATIONS PLANNING UNIT

Such was the background against which the company set up at the end of 1963 a small planning team within the personnel department at head office. The new unit, Employee Relations Planning (ERP), consisted of three people. The leader had worked in Shell UK Limited for many years and had latterly been personnel manager at both Stanlow and Shell Haven. His colleagues were a personnel man from Stanlow and an economist from Shell Chemical Company Limited.

Their terms of reference were to divorce themselves from current refinery affairs and to produce long-term plans for dealing with the problems at shop-floor level. They were asked to take into consideration any repercussions the long-term plans might have on the junior levels of staff. No time limit was set and the team was allowed absolute freedom in deciding how to carry out its task. The results of its efforts are described in Chapter 4.

STREAMLINING NUMBERS

Independently of the long-term planning activities of ERP, it was decided by the company management in April 1964 to carry out an overall reduction of approximately 18 per cent in the number of hourly paid employees at the refineries. The percentage was considerably higher at Shell Haven (26 per cent) than at the other two refineries because of the difficulties of reducing numbers there through normal wastage in previous years. There were also smaller-scale reductions in the number of certain categories of staff.

The reasons for this decision were the growing competitive pressures to reduce operating costs and the results of recent surveys which showed clearly that Shell UK Limited's refineries were considerably over-manned compared with similar Shell refineries elsewhere in the world, particularly in the US.

As previous history, especially at Shell Haven, had demonstrated that the possibility of securing union agreement to such drastic reductions was negligible, they were announced as a unilateral decision by the management. However, the method of achieving the required reductions was to be by means of a voluntary redundancy programme. Each employee who volunteered to leave would receive a generous separation payment, geared to his length of service.

Furthermore, the unions were invited to enter into negotiation with the company on an agreement designed to increase flexibility and reduce demarcation restrictions, so as to make it possible to run the refineries with the considerably smaller workforce.

The company's decision to reduce numbers in this way and on this scale came as a considerable shock to most employees. A union representative at Stanlow spoke of "being bitten by a sheep." Since the war, redundancy was extremely rare in the refineries and had been limited to a few clear cases of the termination of specific activities.

There was strong union resistance to the proposals, but nevertheless the target reductions were achieved by means of the voluntary redundancy scheme at all locations within six months. In due course, moreover, most people came to accept that the new manning levels were adequate to permit the safe and effective operation of the refineries.

The negotiations to secure increased flexibility and relaxation of demarcation restrictions made some progress but were completed only at Ardrossan. At Shell Haven and Stanlow final agreement was not reached and the negotiations were abandoned by mutual consent in 1966.

So far as staff employees were concerned, the voluntary redundancy scheme was applied to unionised staff in the laboratories. For reasons which seemed good at the time, however, non-unionised staff were individually selected for redundancy, rather than being invited to volunteer under the scheme. Although individuals selected for redundancy received more generous separation payments than those who volunteered, it became clear later that the differentiation in treatment was widely resented among the staff. Also resented by some was the fact that the voluntary scheme had resulted in many of the best employees' deciding to leave.

Effects of the streamlining exercise
From the point of view of long-term planning, the effects of the exercise were very mixed.

On the positive side, it had successfully introduced more appropriate and competitive levels of manpower. The need to incorporate large-scale reductions in numbers in the long-term plans was therefore avoided. It had made a first break in the web of restrictive practices which at Shell Haven were stifling productivity and threatening the possibility of future expansion there. It had demolished the idea that, irrespective of the level of efficiency or productivity, a job with Shell was a job for life, provided people "kept their noses clean." It had, therefore, perhaps prepared people for further changes in the future.

On the negative side, the exercise had given the morale of many people, including some quite senior staff, a severe jolt. Few, if any, would have argued that the reductions in manpower were not justified, or necessary. But there were many misgivings about the way in which they had been achieved. There was resentment about the lack of prior consultation and the different treatment applied to non-unionised staff.

In some quarters, existing distrust of management's motives and intentions was intensified. The result of this was to be seen later in the reception given to the company's long-term plans by the craft shop stewards at Shell Haven.

The demolition of the old "Joe Shell" image had its greatest effect on the longer-service employees. Along with it tended to be demolished also the tradition of loyalty to the company, which had provided a form of motivation, a sense of obligation to do a fair day's work.

The largely unsuccessful attempt to bargain greater flexibility and less demarcation with the unions lessened the chances of future productivity bargaining of this kind, because people became weary of the attempt. It demonstrated that a completely new approach to productivity bargaining would be necessary if it was to succeed.

Chapter 3

Background of Tavistock Institute of Human Relations

The Tavistock Institute was not involved in ERP's initial planning work which was to lead to the development programme in Shell UK Limited. As will be clear from later chapters, however, their subsequent involvement in the planning and implementation of the programme was a vital factor in its success. The statement of objectives and management philosophy, which was to play a key role in the whole project, was based upon concepts developed and introduced by them. It is, therefore, useful to review in this chapter some of the major research studies and projects which the Institute was involved in before the company approached them in 1965 to show how these projects had contributed to the development of their theories and concepts.

The Institute was established in 1946 by a group of social scientists who had worked together in the army in the Second World War, solving special problems which could not be dealt with by the normal military machinery. Most of the original group had been members of the Tavistock Clinic before the war, so that their work was initially psychoanalytically oriented. As the problems they were asked to tackle became more complex, the team was joined by people from other disciplines: psychologists, sociologists and anthropologists. At the end of the war, the team decided to continue their efforts to bring their specialised interdisciplinary knowledge to bear in a practical way on the problems of society, and thus the Institute was founded.

Examples of the tasks on which the wartime group collaborated were the setting up of group selection board procedures for officer-candidates and the planning and establishment of civil resettlement units through which large numbers of repatriated prisoners of war volunteered to pass on their way back to civilian life.

THE GLACIER PROJECT

The first long-term project in which Tavistock were involved after the war was the collaborative study of the dynamics of inter- and intra-group relations at all levels of an industrial concern, carried out in the Glacier Metal Company Limited. The results of this work have been well documented, both by the leader of the Tavistock team, Elliott Jaques (1951), and by the Chairman and Managing Director of the company, Wilfred Brown (1960). The formal study lasted for three years, from 1948 to 1951, after which Elliott Jaques continued to work with the company in a consultant capacity.

The initial focus of the study was Wilfred Brown's concern with the arbitrary nature of executive authority in the organisation and the need, as he saw it, to create a system in which the exercise of authority should be democratically sanctioned within the company. Such a system had to be created, he argued, if work people were to be more committed to actions decided upon and if the gap caused by the "split at the bottom of the executive chain" (that is, between foreman and worker) was to be closed.

The study led, therefore, as a preliminary step, to an attempt at a precise definition of organisational concepts, roles and functions, including the identification, for example, of the three systems—the executive, the representative and the legislative—which must co-exist in an organisation although seldom explicitly recognised.

An advanced and sophisticated form of joint consultation was designed, replacing the normal tow-sided works council with a complex system which involved the representation of three different levels of management. The principle of unanimous decision making was established, and the works council was set the task, in its legislative council role, of drawing up an agreed set of personnel policies and procedures for the company.

In spite, however, of these impressive achievements in terms of creating an organisational structure which gave people a democratic voice in the formulation of policy and, through the appeals system, in its implementation, the verdict of Wilfred Brown when he reviewed progress in 1960 was that the "split at the bottom of the executive chain" was regrettably still there.

It seemed that an answer to the problem of the alienation of the worker was not to be found by studying and changing the people-side of the organisation in isolation. Tavistock's further work was to show that many of the problems affecting the people-side (or the social system, as they termed it) had their roots in the technical system and in the actual tasks it required people to carry out. It was therefore essential to study the social system in the context of the technical system if further progress was to be made.

THE COAL MINING STUDIES

Tavistock accordingly sought opportunities to develop research in this area, and became involved in a number of studies in the British coal mines extending from 1950–58. It was during these studies that the term: "socio-technical system" was coined, to describe any typical organisational unit comprising the two inter-dependent parts: a social system. The studies also threw new light on the way in which a unit's performance and productivity could be greatly affected by the degree of appropriateness with which the two parts, the social and the technical, were matched together. Two of the coal studies are reviewed below:

The Longwall method of coal-getting. This was a semi-mechanised system involving automatic coal cutters and a conveyor-belt for filling and loading the coal, which had replaced the old traditional hand-got method. The Longwall method had encountered many difficulties but some changes in manning arrangements had emerged in some pits which were giving more promising results. One purpose of the study was therefore to examine what these changes were and to determine to what extent they might be more generally applicable in other pits. The study included what was the first "socio-technical" analysis of a productive system. In other words, it made a detailed study of the technical system, not merely as background to examining the set-up of the social system, but in order to see how appropriately the two had been related to each other.

In their report on this study, Eric Trist and K W Bamforth (1951) show first how the organisation of work in the old hand-got method was ideally matched to the nature and the demands of the task. The miners had developed over generations a system where small groups of two or three men per shift worked their own narrow face. Every man was capable of doing all the tasks involved in the three main phases of the work, breaking up the coal face ("preparing"), moving the coal to the tubs and filling ("getting"), and then fixing pit props and moving forward to the new coal face ("advancing"). Thus, at whatever phase of the job one shift finished, the next shift picked up the work and carried on. They were self-selecting groups and shared a common wage packet. They needed no external supervision to direct their activities, which was as well, considering the dark, remote and physically cramped conditions in which they worked. Furthermore, as a small, mutually-supporting and autonomous group, they were well suited to withstand the danger and the stress of their underground task.

By contrast, the way in which the work organisation had been set up to deal with the semi-mechanised Longwall method was not at all well suited to the demands and nature of the new technical system. Mechanisation made it possible to work a single long face of up to 200 yards in place of the many short faces of the hand-got method. This meant that as many as forty or fifty men over three shifts were engaged on the face and the quantity of coal to be handled by the system was greatly increased.

Faced with the problem of creating an organisation to cope with this new and more complex situation, management and engineers turned to the conventional pattern of production engineering. Thus each of the three shifts was allocated one of the main phases—"preparing," "getting" and "advancing." Within each shift, the work was further broken down into specialised tasks and men were assigned to a specific task group. There was no self-selection. Each group was paid separately. Responsibility for co-ordination between the task groups and between shifts was not vested in the men, but placed with external supervisors.

The effects of this system of working were damaging both to productivity and to the morale of the men. As they were restricted to, and paid for, a single specialised task, each group tended to concern itself only with its own task, at the expense of the overall objective. Delays and difficulties on one shift would hold up and disrupt the following one. Conflict between task groups, and with supervision whom the men now held responsible for delays, caused high absence and accident rates, and low morale.

The changes in the social system which had begun to emerge in some pits were in the direction of creating groups with more flexible skills who would not be limited to a specific task. The next study goes further and shows how the same Longwall technical system could be operated much more effectively by a social system derived not from production engineering, but from the characteristics of the old hand-got method of mining.

The Durham studies. In studies in the Durham coal mines, Eric Trist and his colleagues located within the same seam, and using the same Longwall technical system, two quite different work organisations. They were able to compare the functioning and effectiveness of the two systems over a period of two years. The results are reported in their book: *Organisational Choice* (1963).

The first system was the conventional Longwall organisation with specialised tasks, described in the previous section. The second, which they called the composite system, had been developed largely by the miners themselves and incorporated many of the features of the old, hand-got working methods. Thus, in the composite system, the men were multi-skilled and able to move from role to role. The group accepted responsibility for the deployment of its members. There was also rotation over shifts, so that no man was pinned to a particular shift or task. Payment was on an overall output basis for the whole group of forty men and divided up by them, usually in equal amounts. Men were thus committed to the overall task, not only to a specific part of it.

The differences in the effectiveness of these two systems, both operating with the same technology in the same seam, were striking, not only in terms of productivity but also of response to stress, as indicated by levels of sickness and absence. For example:

	CONVENTIONAL SYSTEM	COMPOSITE SYSTEM
Productive achievement (as per cent of coal face potential)	78%	95%
Ancillary work at face (hours per man-shift)	1.32	0.03
Per cent of shifts with cycle lag	69%	5%
Absenteeism (per cent of possible shifts):		
no reason given	4.3%	0.4%
sickness or other	8.9%	4.6%
accident	6.8%	3.2%
total	20%	8.2%

Conclusions

The coal mine studies were of great importance and enabled Tavistock to draw the following main theoretical conclusions.

The concept of the socio-technical system. The need to study a production system as a whole and to understand the interrelatedness of all its aspects. Trist and Bamforth wrote: "So close is the relationship between the various aspects, that the social and the psychological can be understood only in terms of the detailed engineering facts and of the way the technological system as a whole behaves in the environment of the underground situation."

The organisation as an open system. In connection with the above, Tavistock argued that it was no longer adequate to consider an organisation as a closed system, sufficiently shut off within its own boundary to enable its problems to be analysed without reference to its external environment. It must be seen as an open system in constant interaction with its environment, and this must be taken into account in the analysis of its problems.

The principle of organisational choice. The importance of matching the social and the technical systems together in the most appropriate way had been conclusively demonstrated. (Tavistock termed this "joint optimisation of the socio-technical system.") This clearly had implications for the design of new systems or the revamping of old ones.

The importance of autonomous groups. It had been demonstrated that when men formed an autonomous group with a degree of responsibility for a major section of the task, where the group set its own target and managed its own internal relationships, the most favourable results were achieved.

Alienation from work. Poor morale and lack of motivation were directly engendered by the type of work role created by the prevailing standards of production engineering which were exemplified in the conventional Longwall system of working. This led Tavistock to develop some general theories on the psychological conditions under which people could be motivated at work. These were to be built into Shell

UK's statement of objectives and philosophy and will be enlarged upon in Chapter 6.

INDIA: TEXTILE MILL STUDY

An opportunity to test out in a completely different industry and environment the theories developed during the coal mine studies arose in 1952. A K Rice (1958) led a Tavistock team invited to investigate the disappointing results in terms of output and damage in a textile company in Ahmedabad, India, following the installation of automatic looms. Studies were carried out over the period 1953–5. They showed that the principle concerning the need to match the social system appropriately to the technical system was as valid in the Indian textile mills, as it had been in the british coal mines.

The mill in question was divided into a number of weaving rooms, each with about 240 looms, set out in banks. As a result of a recent preceding engineering study, the work of tending the looms had been divided into twelve separate and specialist roles: for example, weavers, battery fillers, oilers, fitters, etc. Moreover, each specialist had responsibility for attending to different numbers of looms, so that the task of co-ordinating their efforts—an essential requirement of the technology—was very difficult if not impossible.

When the research team suggested the idea of a group of workers. becoming responsible for a specific bank of looms, it was accepted enthusiastically by the workers, who contributed significantly to the design of a new manning scheme to be tried out on an experimental basis. Essentially, the scheme reduced the number of job categories from twelve to three and completely altered the supervisory pattern. It produced stable groups of workers with responsibility and the necessary skills to maintain a bank of looms in production. It recognised the need for close co-ordination of the workers' efforts to match the interdependence of the different tasks arising on the looms.

The new organisation was highly successful and, after early setbacks had been dealt with, produced results which were considerably more favourable than the previous ones, in terms of production and damage to material, as can be seen from the following production indices for mid-1955.

INDICES	EXISTING TWO SHIFT SYSTEM	EXPERIMENTAL THREE- SHIFT SYSTEM
Loom utilisation	100	131
Efficiency	100	104
Output per man hour	100	187
Total system output	100	121
Damage	100	41

These results remained stable for the several years during which they were monitored.

NORWAY: INDUSTRIAL DEMOCRACY PROJECT

A major opportunity to take part in a project concerned with reducing workers' alienation from their work and making better use of their capabilities arose in Norway in the early 1960s. Tavistock was invited by the Institute for Industrial Social Research in Trondheim to collaborate with a research team led by Einar Thorsrud and commissioned jointly by the national trades union council, the confederation of employers and the Government to help with what later became known as the Norwegian industrial democracy project.

The roots of the project were essentially a general recognition by all parties that as a relatively small economy, Norway needed very much to make more effective use of its human resources; and, more particularly, a growing number of claims from trade unions for worker representation on boards of management, as a means of reducing alienation and increasing productivity.

The research team worked along two paths: an analysis of Norwegian and international experience of various forms of workers' participation in industrial management; and field experiments to improve the level of workers' participation in their own job situation. The team began work in 1962 and the time-scale of the project was seen as about ten years.

The study (Emery and Thorsrud 1964, 1969) on participation at board level indicated that none of the existing methods analysed appeared to do anything towards reducing alienation at shop-floor level, or increasing productivity. Efforts were therefore concentrated on the second alternative: the restructuring of workers' jobs so as to create more autonomous work groups and to give them more responsibility for the performance and the co-ordination of their tasks. As a guide to help with the practical restructuring of jobs the team developed a list of tentative principles for more effective job design, which followed on from Tavistock's findings in the coal mining studies. They are described in a note by Fred Emery which appears in Appendix 2.

The industrial and trades union leaders at national level, who became themselves convinced of the relevance of the approach suggested by the research team—it was based upon socio-technical analysis as a guide to improved job design—formed a joint committee to give overall guidance to the project. With the active support of this committee, several factories were selected for experiments in restructuring jobs, and the consent of the factory managements and the local union representatives obtained.

The factories chosen were in some of the most important sectors of Norwegian industry and were known for having a good record of industrial relations. The idea was that, if successful experiments could be demonstrated in these key sectors, they would serve as examples to encourage other factories to engage in similar experiments. The approach was patterned on earlier work by Fred Emery (1958) in the Australian agricultural industry, which had shown that in order to spread new practices over a very wide area, it was necessary to demonstrate their effectiveness in trial sites and then to establish net works of influential leaders who would press for their adoption in other places.

Metal-working factory

The first experiment took place in the wire-drawing plant of a large engineering concern. Members of the research team carried out a socio-technical analysis of the plant in the early part of 1964. This led to recommendations for changes in the method of manning the machines, which were discussed by all the people concerned, and put into effect in part of the plant on an experimental basis.

The analysis showed that the existing system of manning was ill-suited to the requirements of the technical system. Each wire-drawing machine was tended by one operator. When the machine was functioning satisfactorily, he had virtually nothing to do and the job was dull and boring. Occasionally, however, if the wire broke, the operator would need to act quickly to stop the machine, and then disentangle the wire, weld the ends together, and get it running smoothly again. During this period of intense activity and stress, he would normally

D

receive no help from the other operators, even although they were virtually unoccupied at the time. Each operator was paid on piece-rates individually negotiated with the foreman.

The proposed experimental changes included creating a team of operators who would be jointly responsible for running a number of machines. The team was to be left to develop its own method of working. There was to be some modification of the layout, so that team members could have easier access to their group of machines. They would receive an incentive bonus for any production above the average for the machines involved.

The changes were agreed, with some reservations: for example, the men insisted that the old rule of one man per machine should still apply, although the recommendation had envisaged the team operating more machines than it had men.

Nevertheless, the experiment took place and proved that significant improvements in productivity could be achieved with the new system of manning. Moreover, many of the operators who had been sceptical about the whole idea of working in groups came to agree that working in a team was more satisfying.

The major problem which arose was the effect of the increased productivity on the pay packets of some of the operators involved in the experiment. They had begun to earn more than the most skilled workers in the plant. This caused much unrest and resentment, and resulted in the suspension of the experiment before the end of the agreed trial period.

The two major conclusions which emerged, therefore, from this study were:

1   Further confirmation that the principles of job design developed by Tavistock could be applied to improve productivity and increase job satisfaction
2   Greater recognition that traditional wage systems and procedures represented serious obstacles to introducing changes in manning arrangements and working methods

Paper and pulp factory
The second experiment began in late 1964 in the chemical pulp department of a paper and pulp factory. Unlike the first factory, the technology here was new and sophisticated. The socio-technical analysis carried

out by the research team demonstrated, however, that the production process was often out of control, in the sense that it was outside the defined quality control limits. Whilst this was not reflected in the end-quality of the product, it did involve high costs. It meant that some of the key process variables were not being controlled by the operators and some of them had not in fact been identified.

The recommendations for change were, therefore, concerned with measures which would enable the operators to get more information about the state of the process and thus to set their own performance targets and learn from their errors.

Specific proposals were accordingly made for the setting up of an information centre in the department to show process developments over the shifts; the training of operators for more flexible roles; improved logging of process data; and a bonus related to quality control, over which operators could now exert more influence.

A feature of the project was the setting up of an action committee which included an operator and an assistant foreman to be responsible for implementation of the action programme.

Another feature was the opposition to the project of some sections of employees. At one stage, in 1965, for example, a proposal from some shop floor employees to have the whole project abandoned was only defeated by a narrow majority vote. In spite of such difficulties, however, changes were gradually introduced and improvements slowly made themselves apparent. An indication of the success of the project was that by early 1966, in response to demands from the employees, preparations were in hand to start a second project in another part of the factory.

Some conclusions which emerged from the paper and pulp study were therefore:

1   The identification of information handling as the key capability required to control a sophisticated process technology
2   The need to seek the involvement of all organisational levels in the change project, in order to avoid resistance and opposition
3   The value of an action committee including men whose jobs are being changed
4   The need for patience and perseverance in effecting changes of this nature

Tavistock were also involved during the early 1960s in a number of additional projects in other organisations as diverse, for example, as the national transport undertaking in Dublin (van Beinum 1966) and the building industry in Britain (Higgin and Jessop 1965). These projects all contributed to the building up of the theoretical and practical know-how which the Institute would bring to the development programme of Shell UK Limited.

Part Two
A COMPANY DEVELOPMENT PROGRAMME IS PROPOSED

Chapter 4

Diagnosis of the
Problem and Proposals for Action

The employee relations planning unit—ERP—started its work at the beginning of 1964. General expectations in the company at that time were that it would produce some form of plan for productivity bargaining. Certainly the focus of attention was the problem of how to increase productivity at shop-floor level, where some dramatic improvement was clearly needed.

Protected from the day to day pressures of the tactical industrial relations situation, the ERP team were able to read, reflect, visit other companies in the UK, the Netherlands and North America and build up their ideas. It became clear to them that the problem of shop-floor productivity could not be looked at in isolation: it was only part of a larger-scale problem.

They relied most heavily upon their own experience of working in the company and that of their colleagues in the refineries. But they were impressed and encouraged to find that their own experience-based views on the nature and scale of the problem seemed to be supported by the writings and findings of the social scientists—some of whose books they now at last found time to read.

At this stage, with the exception of the Glacier project, the team was unaware of the work which had been done by the Tavistock Institute, as summarised in Chapter 3. The Glacier results were looked at, but the approach did not seem to promise any solution to the company's problem. Most relevant at that time seemed to be people like A H Maslow (1954) and Fred Herzberg (1959) with their research and theories about motivation and the causes of satisfaction or dissatisfac-

41

tion in the work situation; and Douglas McGregor (1960) with his notion of theory X and theory Y assumptions about the nature of man, and his arguments in favour of a participative style of management. Further reference to this area of work is included in the quotations from ERP's report which follow.

DIAGNOSIS OF THE PROBLEM

The team reported its diagnosis of the problem and its proposals for action in January, 1965. Two major problem areas were identified: first, the unfavourable or negative attitudes which many hourly paid employees had towards their jobs and towards the company; and, second, the many restrictive and inappropriate terms and conditions of employment which had been incorporated over the years in the trade union agreements and with which managers were only too familiar. It was suggested that the two problems were interlinked and that until a more favourable general working climate and more positive attitudes could be induced, there were limits to what could be achieved through conventional productivity bargaining. ERP's report put it in the following terms:

> We consider that there are definite limitations to the amount of progress we can hope to make in the future in achieving greater productivity by more effective use of manpower through conventional bargaining tactics, given the present climate of relationships at Shell Haven and Stanlow. . . . In the present climate it is inevitable that there will continue to be a barrier of opposition and mistrust on the part of many men. . . . Fundamentally the men are not committed to the company's objective and the most we can hope for is that they will honour the bargains they have entered into. Experience at Fawley, for example, has been that the "Blue Book" bargains have been honoured but that the men are not prepared to extend their co-operation to cover any work not specifically mentioned in the agreement. (Flanders, 1964.)
>
> It is our opinion that in order to open up the way to a much higher productive level of effort, it is necessary to go beyond conventional bargaining, which is essentially a matter of attempting to push the barrier back with the aid of financial inducements and to attempt to remove, or break through the barrier itself. We should therefore make it our long-term policy to secure a funda-

mental change in attitude on the part of employees to the point where, in a climate of mutual trust and confidence between men and management, it becomes possible for them to commit themselves fully to the company objective of having its work carried out with maximum efficiency and productivity. It is undoubtedly true that only with such personal commitment to the job in hand, will the full potential of a man's capability be realised and there is ample evidence that, under present circumstances, only a small proportion of this potential is being utilised. It is appreciated of course that the attainment of this long-term objective will be extremely difficult and, indeed, may never be completely achieved. Nevertheless, we consider that any intermediate plans which we decide to introduce should be consistent with and help progress towards this long-term aim.

The point was then made that, in large part, the attitude of the hourly paid employees had been formed over the years by the way in which they had been managed. In seeking to change shop-floor attitudes, therefore, it was essential first to secure changes in attitude among supervisors and managers:

The attitude of mind of the hourly paid employees cannot, of course, be looked at in isolation, since it depends to a very significant extent on the attitude encountered at all levels of supervisory and management staff. We consider, therefore, that before we can expect any change in attitude among unionised employees, we must attempt to secure changes in attitude among supervisors and management.

It was suggested that a more participative management style would need to be adopted if people down the line were to become more effectively motivated:

The effectiveness of different types of management style (e.g. authoritarian, permissive, etc) is a subject on which a great deal of research has been carried out and where there is a large measure of agreement among the experts. The conclusion reached is broadly that the historical authoritarian system of management by control through rewards and punishments is no longer appropriate or effective today since the "punishments" available to management no longer carry any weight. Effective management in modern industry can only be practised by the consent of those managed.

It is held therefore that the most effective form of management is one where at each level from the top downwards, positive efforts are made to involve each subordinate fully in the work he is carrying out. This requires that each boss should take his subordinates into his confidence, encourage them to contribute to and participate in any decisions which will affect them or their work, help them to set their own goals or targets and leave them free to carry them out. In short, to make it possible for them, with his guidance, to commit themselves and their energies wholeheartedly to the objectives of the company in the tasks they undertake.

Such a management style can be contrasted, for example, with one where a subordinate receives instructions from his boss in ignorance of the background or justification for the task demanded and is therefore personally uncommitted to carrying out the task effectively and fails to devote his whole enthusiasm and energy towards it.

The management style recommended involves true delegation to subordinates as opposed to a system where the subordinate, having been assigned a task, is subjected to constant checking and control; by encouraging a man to set his own targets and, in conjunction with his boss, to review his own progress, conditions are created where the man can grow and develop in the job instead of, as under the other conditions described, becoming dissatisfied and frustrated in the job.

These findings tie in with another line of research carried out over the years into the motivation of individuals in industry. Here the conclusion reached by a number of researchers is that there are a number of factors which motivate people to work and that these factors can be broadly divided into two levels or categories. First, there are what have been called the "hygiene" factors, that is, money, working conditions and security. These are extremely important in the sense that if they are not adequately looked after, men will become dissatisfied, suffer poor morale and put in minimum effort. On the other hand, these factors, when adequately looked after, do not act as positive motivators towards optimum effort. This is more the function of the second level of positive motivational factors which can come into effect once the hygiene factors are adequately catered for. These are interest in the job, prestige and recognition as an individual, the opportunity to develop one's own ability and to accept responsibility.

These are the factors which really motivate people to give of their best and it is clear that the style of management advocated is best suited to provide opportunities for subordinates to be motivated in this way: the optimum situation being that through the personal satisfaction they derive, subordinates identify their own personal goals with achievement of company objectives and devote their whole energy to both. It should perhaps be stressed that this style by no means equates with "soft" management. The boss (at the appropriate level) still takes the decisions. Indeed, this system, whilst leading to true delegation and the consequent more rapid development of the subordinate, will also make weak links or ineffective subordinates more conspicuous. Another point to be recognised is that this management style is not "new" in the sense that some managers already use it to some extent with success at the present time. On the whole, however, within the company at present there is no explicit recognition that the style of management advocated is effective, nor that the motivational factors which it brings into play are the really important ones from the point of view of company productivity. Up till now, the main emphasis has undoubtedly been placed on a system of management by control and on the use of financial reward and opportunity of advancement as motivators.

It is proposed therefore that given agreement in principle at management level, we should embark on a planned effort to introduce a system of management on the lines described.

ACTION PROPOSALS

Twin lines of action were proposed to deal with the two main problem areas identified:

1 Attitude change. The method suggested for bringing about a change of attitude was that management should adopt a more participative style. It was proposed therefore that the ERP team should produce a draft statement of objectives and management philosophy which, if accepted by company management as appropriate, would then serve as a focal point for discussion and debate by groups of managers and supervisors down the line and throughout the organisation. It was suggested that in the long term, such a dissemination process would bring about the desired change in attitudes at the shop-floor level.

Two further proposals were made in connection with the attitude change programme. First, it was suggested by ERP that outside assistance from social scientists should be sought in the task of drafting the philosophy statement and in its subsequent dissemination. The company did not itself possess the skills and experience to handle the sort of dissemination conferences which were envisaged, nor to deal with the problems which an attitude change programme could be expected to encounter. Second, it was recommended that the company's system of performance appraisal should be modified to bring it into line with the participative style of management now advocated. Thus provision should be made for achievement targets to be agreed between the subordinate and his boss, and for his performance to be reviewed in the light of such targets, rather than judged in terms of his boss's largely subjective impressions.

2 *Productivity bargaining.* To deal with the unsatisfactory aspects of the terms and conditions of employment for unionised employees, it was recommended that the ground should be carefully prepared for comprehensive productivity bargains with the unions. It was suggested that pending discussions with the unions, and whilst the attitude change programme was in operation, a number of study teams should be set up to investigate in depth the implications of all the changes which the company would hope to see introduced as a result of eventual bargains with the unions. ERP suggested that the company should be aiming for such changes as: staff status for all hourly paid employees; annual salaries in place of hourly rates; abolition of overtime payments; increased flexibility and a reduction in demarcation restrictions. By setting up study teams, when the time for bargaining arrived a great deal of objective data would be available on all the critical issues.

INTERACTION OF TWIN ACTION PROPOSALS

The two lines of action recommended were seen as interlinked and complementary. The diagram in Figure 4:1 shows schematically how it was hoped they would together serve to combat the problems at shop-floor level, and bring about higher levels of motivation and productivity. Thus it was thought that the attitude change programme would have a favourable effect on the general climate of the work place and on people's attitudes. This should enhance the chances of successful joint development of productivity bargains. Satisfactory bargains with the unions by eliminating, for example, overtime payments, would in turn make it simpler to introduce further changes on the shop floor, such as different working methods or different job structures which, it was hoped, would flow from the adoption of a more participative management philosophy.

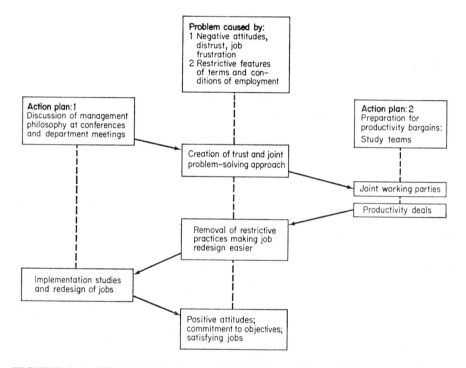

FIGURE 4:1 SCHEMATIC PLAN OF IDEAL INTERACTION OF ACTION PROPOSALS IN SOLVING THE PROBLEM AT SHOP-FLOOR LEVEL

Chapter 5

Acceptance of Proposals

First reactions to ERP's report were mixed. Some managers were very supportive; others, particularly those who had anticipated proposals for a straightforward plan, were somewhat sceptical. There were a few who felt that after only a relatively short period away from refinery life, the team members' feet had lost contact with the ground.

In March 1965, the managing director held a two-day meeting of his full management team, together with the management of Shell Chemical Company Limited. The purpose of the meeting was to work through ERP's diagnosis and proposals in detail and to decide what action, if any, should be taken on their recommendations. This was, therefore, the first of three critical decision-making meetings which the company's top management team was to hold within the space of twelve months and which were to determine whether the development programme should be planned and launched and the way it should grow.

In the course of the meeting, which had been highly structured, with a detailed agenda paper indicating all the points on which decisions were needed, there was ample opportunity for examination of both diagnosis and action plans. One statement in the ERP report which caused some managers concern was: "Effective management in modern industry can only be practised by the consent of those managed." It was explained that this did not mean or imply that in order to get anything done, managers must request the consent of each individual to carry out a particular instruction. It simply meant that unless there was a general acceptance of management's right to give instructions in any area, such instructions would not be carried out effectively. At worst, there could be open rejection of the instructions, for example, through a withdrawal of labour. At best, people would go through the motions, but the work would not get done effectively.

The outcome of the meeting was a general acceptance of ERP's diagnosis of the problem, which was considered to be valid; and the endorsement of all the proposals for action. Specifically the meeting decided that:

1   It should be a long-term objective of the company to secure an improvement in attitudes
2   Changes in management attitudes were necessary and should be initiated without delay
3   A participative management philosophy and style, as advocated in the report, should be introduced into all managerial and supervisory ranks, starting at the top
4   ERP should produce a detailed statement of objectives and management philosophy for discussion by the management team
5   ERP should find themselves appropriate social science assistance for the drafting of the document. The question of social science help in subsequent phases of the programme was left open for future consideration
6   Detailed proposals should be drawn up for a system of target-setting and performance review, which was agreed in principle
7   ERP should prepare detailed terms of reference for the proposed study teams who would be making exploratory studies of the areas likely to be affected by productivity bargaining

The first critical step had been taken and the next management decision point had been set up: it would be taken after discussion of the statement of objectives and philosophy which ERP were now required to produce.

As a result of this meeting also, the management of Shell Chemical Company Limited decided that they would like their employees at Stanlow and Shell Haven chemical plants to participate fully in the programme. They reserved their judgement about the remainder of their organisation.

SECURING SOCIAL SCIENCE ASSISTANCE

After the meeting, ERP produced a work programme showing the tasks envisaged over the following twelve months. On the one side, the drafting of the statement of objectives and philosophy, and its dissemination through a series of conferences, resulting in a start on implementation measures, as yet unspecified. On the other, the establishment of study teams for whom terms of reference were now laid down, leading to the beginning of joint discussions with union representatives.

Meanwhile, in parallel with seeking social science help, a first attempt was made to draft the philosophy statement. The team were forced to admit to themselves, however, that their efforts amounted to no more than a reasonably elegant piece of exhortation: a plea for a participative management style which lacked rational foundation and logical structure. It was clear that the statement would need to be more firmly based on reason and logic if it were to stand up to the rigorous testing it would undoubtedly be submitted to by managers throughout the company. The exercise served, therefore, to reinforce the need for outside assistance with this task.

How to find social science help

Whilst fully convinced of the need, ERP and others in the company found themselves rather ignorant about how to engage appropriate social science assistance. There appeared to be no register of resources available in the field. They decided, therefore, to make individual approaches to a number of prominent social scientists in the UK academic field. The method of approach was to send them a copy of the ERP report and work programme and then to meet for a discussion.

In each case, the outcome of these discussions was similar. The company's intentions were approved, with varying degrees of enthusiasm, but none of the social scientists approached had sufficient time available to assist with the project. In spite of this, the discussions were valuable. In addition to a specific recommendation to approach the Tavistock Institute, they provided an opportunity to expose the proposed change programme to a range of informed social science opinion, and confirmation that the proposals made sense. They also gave ERP a clearer recognition of the scale of social science help which would be needed for a project of the complexity envisaged.

THE TAVISTOCK INSTITUTE—HUMAN RESOURCES CENTRE

An approach was duly made to the Tavistock Institute. The Institute was composed of five centres whose domains ranged from family and community psychiatry at one end to operational research at the other. The company's approach was to the Human Resources Centre group, whose chairman at that time was Eric Trist. Future use in this book of the term "Tavistock" will therefore refer specifically to this group.

A meeting with Eric Trist and his colleagues in May 1965 showed a high degree of mutual interest and compatibility of objectives. Tavistock were impressed with the scope of the company's plans and with their relevance to their own previous work in this field. They felt they could contribute theoretically to the launching and development of the project and, on the basis of their practical knowledge and experience, lend support at times of set-back and disappointment which, they warned, would inevitably arise in the course of such a large-scale undertaking. Furthermore, they could make sufficient resources immediately available to work on it.

Trial period

At the suggestion of Tavistock, it was agreed that the company would engage their services for a trial period of three to four months, beginning in July 1965. This would allow sufficient time for an orientation programme, the drafting of the statement of objectives and philosophy and its acceptance or rejection by the company's management team.

The working arrangements would be flexible. Four senior members of the Tavistock group would make themselves available during the trial period for whatever time they were needed: the leader, Eric Trist; Fred Emery, Gurth Higgin and Harold Bridger. At the end of the trial period, both the company and Tavistock would be in a position to decide whether they wished to continue the collaboration.

Orientation

The first concern of Eric Trist and his colleagues was to explore for themselves the company's organisation and technical system, its objectives, its boundaries and its links with the outside world. Gurth Higgin made a visit to Shell's refinery in the Netherlands, at Pernis, in order to get a first-hand impression of the technology, of which, as yet, Tavistock had no intimate knowledge. It was better that they should learn something about this from somewhere independent of the UK locations with which they would soon become involved.

Their normal link with the company was the ERP team. By channelling all contacts and communications through ERP, it was possible to co-ordinate activities and plot where the project was moving. More-

E

over, Tavistock saw it as an important task, not only to feed in to the company as much of their own knowledge and experience as possible, but also to help people inside the company acquire social science skills and expertise. The ERP team members were the logical people with whom to start this process and Tavistock set out to build a close collaborative relationship with them. From the beginning of the trial period, therefore, Tavistock and ERP established a pattern of joint discussions and joint planning meetings which was to continue throughout the project.

Visits were arranged for the Tavistock members to each of the refineries and they met all the senior executives in the company's head office. In addition to carrying out their own appreciation of the company's situation, they were concerned to assess the validity of the problem diagnosis on which ERP had based its action proposals.

ERP's assumptions about the level of morale and motivation among shop floor people, for example, had been based on its members' own working experience and their extensive contacts with hourly paid employees. The possibility of conducting an attitude survey to get some objective data on the subject had been considered in 1964 but had been rejected because it was feared the results would have been unduly influenced by the run-down in numbers imposed by the company in that year.

By the end of their orientation programme, after discussions with a wide range of people in head office and at the refineries, Tavistock were satisfied that the diagnosis appeared to be valid. The next task was to produce a draft of the objectives and philosophy statement.

Part Three
DISSEMINATING
A MANAGEMENT PHILOSOPHY

Chapter 6

The Statement of Objectives and Philosophy

The statement was to be the focal point of the whole development programme. It was to set out exactly what the objectives of the company were and the philosophy, or principles, which would serve as guidelines to managers when taking decisions. This was felt to be essential if the long-term aim of changing unfavourable attitudes and securing a higher level of commitment to the company's objectives was to be achieved. It was also necessary to give employees the opportunity to discuss the statement so that they could either accept or reject the objectives and principles it set out. It was hoped that both would be endorsed by employees at all levels in the organisation and that, as a result, they would in time be encouraged and motivated to devote their energies to putting the philosophy into practice. Acceptance would imply, in broad terms, consent to manage and be managed in accordance with the principles set out in the statement and in pursuit of the stated objectives.

DRAFTING THE STATEMENT

Although it was not immediately apparent, the theories and concepts which Tavistock had developed as a result of the sort of work described in Chapter 3, fitted exactly into the picture the company wished to create. Moreover, they provided the firm logical structure which the statement needed and which had been lacking from ERP's own first efforts at drafting.

The statement was drafted by a small team: Fred Emery of Tavistock

55

and two members of ERP. They had available to them a set of company objectives which had recently been drawn up by the management team. They also had available the experience which all the Tavistock members had gained as a result of the orientation programme and their own analysis of the company system. Working only part of the time, the task was completed within a month.

Purpose and criteria

The drafting team first established for themselves the purpose the statement was to serve and the criteria its contents would have to meet.

It was agreed that the statement was not intended to serve as a public relations document for use outside the company; nor was it in any way to be used for industrial relations purposes, to supersede or replace existing agreements with the trade unions. It was intended to be a working document which would provide practical guidance in the management and operation of the company. Two main drafting criteria were established:

Validity. The contents of the statement would have to be seen as valid by all employees and have some relevance to the actual carrying out of their tasks in the various areas of the company's activity. Furthermore, its contents should continue to be valid and relevant over a reasonable span of time—five to ten years—by taking into account any developments such as those in technology which could be foreseen within that time span.

Appropriateness. The principles, or values, written into the statement would have to be appropriate to the nature of the company's main activities—that is, refining.

Jargon

The first draft was tested out informally with a number of people at various levels and in different functions. First reactions to the document were often doubtful, since the concepts embodied in it were new to people and some of the wording caused problems. However, after a process of discussion and clarification, and some minor modification of the text, everyone consulted was satisfied that the contents of the document were both valid and appropriate.

Tavistock and ERP agreed that no attempt should be made to "simplify" the document by eliminating or paraphrasing the jargon. The result of such an attempt would, they felt, be a loss of some of the statement's meaning and power. Furthermore, it was intended that the document would never be used as a "hand-out" for employees to read without the opportunity for debate and discussion. Experience had shown that discussion was essential to bring out the full meaning and implications of the document and that in the course of this process, the jargon usually ceased to be a problem.

SUMMARY OF THE STATEMENT'S CONTENTS

The full statement is reproduced in the second half of this chapter. Before reading it, however, it will be helpful to look at its structure, which is shown in Figure 6:1, in conjunction with the summary of its contents which follows, and which highlights the major concepts involved. The main arguments which arose in subsequent discussions of the statement are described in Chapter 7. The statement consisted of seven main sections:

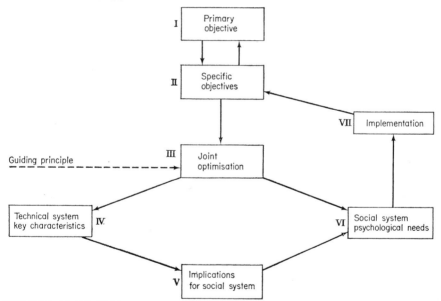

FIGURE 6:1 LOGICAL STRUCTURE OF THE STATEMENT OF OBJECTIVES
AND PHILOSOPHY

1 Primary objective. The company's primary objective is expressed in terms of maximising its contribution to the Group's long-term profitability, insofar as this arises from the efficient use of resources. There follows what could be termed the company's social objective: this involves commitment to two key concepts:

(*a*) That all the resources it uses are "social resources" (that is, are in the last analysis resources of the community), and must be protected and developed as such

(*b*) That the resources must be used to contribute to the satisfaction of the community's needs for products and services

Thus the company commits itself to seeking improved profitability and the creation of new wealth only in ways which will also benefit society —through meeting community needs efficiently and through protecting and developing the social resources it uses.

2   *Specific objectives.* Six specific objectives are spelled out, within the overall framework of the primary objective. Two are operational objectives, concerned with meeting present and future market requirements. The third is related to the company's position in the Group. The last three derive from the commitment to protect and develop resources and are concerned with the development of people, safety and the need to minimise pollution of the environment.

3   *The principle of joint optimisation as a guide to implementation.* The guiding principle to assist the company in pursuing its objectives is the joint optimisation of the social and the technical systems. As described in Chapter 3, joint optimisation means the best possible matching together of the people in any unit and the way their jobs are organised, with the physical equipment and material resources in that unit. The statement of this principle here leads on to an examination of the technical system, and of its implications for the design of the social system.

4   *Key characteristics of the evolving technical system.* Seven fundamental characteristics of the technical system are identified, which are likely to remain unchanged in the foreseeable future, and which must therefore be taken into account in deciding how best to design the social system.

5   *Implications for the social system.* By considering the implications of the key technical characteristics, the most appropriate matching human characteristics are suggested. The most important human task in running process operations is identified as information handling. As this is a skill which cannot be controlled by external supervision, employees must be internally motivated to carry it out efficiently. It follows that the key human characteristics required are responsibility and commitment.

6   *Responsibility and commitment.* This section is concerned with what must be done to create conditions in which people will develop

responsibility and commitment to their tasks. It is suggested that two things are necessary:
  (a) Satisfactory terms and conditions of employment
  (b) Jobs which enable them to satisfy the basic psychological needs of human beings in their work
What are considered to be the main psychological needs are then set out, together with some general principles to be taken into account in redesigning jobs.

7 *Principle of implementation of the philosophy.* The philosophy must be tested in the company through all employees having the opportunity to relate its implications to their own situation. Senior managers have a special responsibility for leading the process of testing and dissemination, and for implementation.

TEXT OF THE STATEMENT

The version of the statement quoted below is dated May 1966, and incorporates a number of additions and improvements which resulted from the first wave of dissemination conferences for senior managers. The key concepts and framework of the statement, however, survived intact from the original draft.

Statement of objectives and management philosophy
1 *Primary objective.* The company is primarily concerned to maximise its contribution to the long-term profitability of the Shell Group insofar as this arises from the efficiency with which it uses the Group's resources of men, money and material.

The resources to which it has legal rights of privileged access are nonetheless part of the total resources of society as a whole and are, in this sense, social resources; the company believes that they must be protected, developed and managed as such. It furthermore believes that its use of these resources must be such as to contribute to meeting society's requirements for products and services.

The company recognises, however, that ultimate discretion for what can be done to maximise Group profitability cannot properly be exercised without having a total picture of the exploration, production, transportation, manufacturing, marketing and research functions. Since the activities of the company lie mainly within the manufacturing function, this makes necessary the statement of its specific objectives in terms of the minimum expenditure of resources appropriate to the discharge of its responsibilities to the Group.

2   Specific objectives. Specifically this commits the company to:

1   Meeting the current market requirements for refined petroleum products with minimum expenditure of total resources per unit of quantity of given quality
2   Ensuring the company's ability to meet emerging market requirements with decreasing expenditure of total resources per unit of quantity of specified quality

An essential task of management is to seek at all times optimal solutions to 1 and 2.
   In addition, the company is specifically committed by its position in the group to:

3   Seeking continually from the Group the power and the information necessary to enable it to meet its responsibilities. In certain circumstances it may be necessary to seek a redefinition of its responsibilities in order that the company's capabilities may be best used on behalf of the Group

Implicit in these three specific objectives and in the fact that the company's resources are part of the total resources of society, are the following additional specific objectives:

4   Creating conditions in which employees at all levels will be encouraged and enabled to develop and to realise their potentialities while contributing towards the company's objectives
5   Carrying out its productive and other operations in such a way as to safeguard the health and safety of its employees and the public
6   Seeking to reduce any interference that may be caused by its activities to the amenities of the community, accepting the measures practised under comparable conditions in British industry as a minimum standard and making use of the expertise and knowledge available within the Group

3   The principle of joint-optimisation as a guide to implementation.
The company must manage both a social system, of people and their

organisation, and a technical system, of physical equipment and re-sources. Optimisation of its overall operations can be achieved only by jointly optimising the operation of these two systems; attempts to optimise the two independently of each other, or undue emphasis upon one of them at the expense or the neglect of the other, must fail to achieve optimisation for the company as a whole.

4 Key characteristics of the evolving technical system. In order to create appropriate conditions for the optimisation of the overall system, it is necessary to design the social system jointly with the technical system recognising that the latter has certain key persistent charac-teristics which must be taken into account. These characteristics are:

1 The company forms part of a complex, science-based industry sub-ject to rapid technical change. This rate of change can be expected to increase in the future.

2 There is a wide measure of flexibility available in all the main processes involved in oil refining, i.e. distillation, conversion and blend-ing. The added value which results from refining operations depends to a high degree upon the skilful use of this flexibility in plant design and operation and the programming of refinery and overall company operations in order to meet variable market requirements from given and variable inputs.

3 The company is capital-intensive and it follows that adequate criteria of overall company performance must be sought mainly in measures of efficiency of plant utilisation. The importance to overall company performance of efficient plant utilisation makes necessary a high degree of plant reliability.

4 The company's refineries are already highly involved with automa-tion and instrumentation. Pressure for a very much higher level of automation and instrumentation arises from the development of new processes and the drive towards optimal use of the flexibility described in 2 above, and the need to improve the ability to control, identify and account for the large number of movements through the tech-nical system at any one time.

5 There is considerable variation in the degree of automation of different operations in the company. Labour-intensive activities exist side by side with highly automated ones. Despite the trends noted in 1 and 4 above, some variation is likely to persist.

6 The company's process operations are carried out on a continuous

twenty-four hours per day, seven-day week basis, but a number of shift teams, while many associated service activities are carried out discontinuously on a day working basis.

7   The refineries and head office are geographically widely separated and within refineries there is considerable dispersion of the various activities. For economic and technical reasons this characteristic is likely to persist.

5   Implications for the social system. The rapid and increasing rate of change in the technical system defined in characteristic 1 creates a special need for new expertise, skills and knowledge at all levels, and new forms of organisation to cope with changing requirements. It also increases the rate at which skills and knowledge are rendered obsolete. The company believes that its objectives in relation to the social nature of its resources commit it to train its employees in new skills and new knowledge where obsolescence of skills and knowledge has resulted from its own or the industry's technical development. These effects require the company to plan for the development of appropriate skills and forms of organisation in parallel with the planning of technical change.

The most significant consequence of characteristics 2, 3, 4, 6 and 7 is that economic production within our process technology is critically dependent upon people effectively dealing with information yielded by the technical system and contributing the most appropriate information to the control and guidance of that system. Some of these informational flows are confined to individuals who take information from the technical system and feed back guidance directly into it. Other informational flows must be carried at any one time by a network of many people at many different organisational levels. The effectiveness of this social informational network depends upon the recognition by all those involved in its design and operation that it is made up of people and is therefore affected by the factors that influence human behaviour.

The wide geographical dispersion of the refineries and the extensive layout within the refineries themselves present an impediment to effective communications. This makes it even more necessary for the company to design efficient informational flows.

A further consequence of characteristic 3, namely the need for a high degree of plant reliability, is that economic production is also highly dependent upon the application of craft skills and knowledge.

In information handling, and to a large degree in the exercise of craft skills, the problem is to avoid lapses of attention and errors in observing, diagnosing and communicating or acting upon information. Information handling work in the refining industry is such that lapses and errors are likely to result in heavy costs, both from delay in recognising errors and taking corrective action and from the nature of the equipment and the processes involved. The only promising way of avoiding these faults is for the individual to be internally motivated to exercise responsibility and initiative. Any external control can only act after the error has occurred or had its effect.

In contrast, in those jobs where the main human contribution is manual labour, there is some choice as to how control may be achieved. Although optimal control requires internal motivation, the shortcomings associated with mainly manual tasks do not normally result in heavy costs and it is possible to achieve an economic degree of control by external incentives and supervision. For these reasons the exercise of personal responsibility and initiative in such work, although desirable, may be considered less significant.

However, the manual jobs in the refineries (characteristic 5) exist mainly amongst service activities ancillary to the operating and engineering activities which are central to the task of oil refining. It is considered essential that the company's philosophy should be appropriate to the nature of these central activities. For those activities of a different nature it may be necessary to modify them through technical developments, e.g. the introduction of mechanisation or automation, or to develop other social systems appropriate to them, in keeping with the values of the company's philosophy.

Despite the complication arising from characteristic 5 therefore, the major implication of this group of technical characteristics emerges as the need to develop a high level of personal responsibility and initiative.

6 Responsibility and commitment. People cannot be expected to develop within themselves and to exercise the level of responsibility and initiative that is required unless they can be involved in their task and unless, in the long run, it is possible to develop commitment to the objectives served by their task.

The company recognises that it cannot expect its employees at all levels to develop adequate involvement and commitment spontaneously or in response to mere exhortation. It must set out to create the conditions under which such commitment may develop.

The work of social scientists has shown that the creation of such conditions cannot be achieved simply by the provision of satisfactory terms of service, including remuneration. The provision of such terms of service is essential, but is not in itself sufficient; for involvement and commitment at all levels it is necessary to go beyond this, to meet the general psychological requirements that men have of their work.

The following are some of the psychological requirements that relate to the content of a job:

1   The need for the content of the work to be reasonably demanding of the individual in terms other than those of sheer endurance, and for it to provide some variety

2   The need for an individual to know what his job is and how he is performing in it

3   The need to be able to learn on the job and go on learning

4   The need for some area of decision making where the individual can exercise his discretion

5   The need for some degree of social support and recognition within the organisation

6   The need for an individual to be able to relate what he does and what he produces to the objectives of the company and to his life in the community

7   The need to feel that the job leads to some sort of desirable future which does not necessarily imply promotion

These requirements exist in some form for the large majority of men and at all levels of employment. Their relative significance, however, will clearly vary from individual to individual and it is not possible to provide for their fulfilment in the same way for all kinds of people. Similarly, different jobs will provide varying degrees of opportunity for the fulfilment of particular requirements.

They cannot generally be met, however, simply by redesigning individual jobs. Most tasks involve more than one person and, in any case, all jobs must be organisationally related to the company's objectives. If the efforts to meet the above requirements for individuals are not to be frustrated, the company must observe certain principles in developing its organisational form. Thus, the individual must know not only what he is required to do, but also the way in which his work ties in with what others are doing, the part he plays in the communications network, and the limits within which he has genuine discretionary powers. Furthermore, the individual's responsibilities should be defined in terms of objectives to be pursued; although procedural rules are necessary for co-ordination, they must be reviewed regularly in the light of experience gained in pursuing these objectives.

Responsibility and authority must go hand in hand in order to avoid situations in which people are delegated responsibility but do not have the means to exercise it. Likewise, the company must be ready to re-define responsibilities where there are capabilities which are unused.

Not least, the company must seek to ensure that the distribution of status and reward is consistent with the level of responsibility carried by the individual.

In following this course the company will seek the fullest involvement of all employees and will make the best use of available knowledge and experience of the social sciences.

7 Principle of implementation of the philosophy. The effective implementation and communication of the philosophy throughout the company can be achieved only if its mode of implementation manifests the spirit of the philosophy. Verbal or written communication alone will not suffice; it is essential that all employees be enabled to relate the philosophy to themselves by participating in the implementation of the philosophy in their particular parts of the company.

A special burden of responsibility must rest with the senior managers, who alone are in a position to exercise the leadership and provide the necessary impetus to translate the philosophy into a living reality. Starting with their commitment, it will be possible to involve progressively the other levels of the employees in searching out the implications for themselves. As the philosophy begins to shape the activities of the company it will be able more effectively to pursue its objectives.

The reactions of the company's top management to the statement are described in the following chapter.

Chapter 7

Management Reactions to the Statement

The most important test the draft statement had to face was the detailed examination it received from the company's top management team. Unless the document was accepted by them the attitude-change programme would clearly not be launched. For this purpose a three-day residential conference was arranged in October 1965 at the Selsdon Park hotel near London. Present were the managing director, his functional heads of departments and the general managers and their deputies from the refineries. Tavistock and ERP were there as advisers. With the managing director in the chair, the group worked through the document sentence by sentence, testing its validity and appropriateness to the company. The timetable was arranged to allow the afternoons free on the first two days, with working sessions before and after the evening meal. Informal discussions then carried on until late in the night.

The whole of the document provoked intensive discussion. It raised some new issues and it focused a new light on old issues. Below are described some of the major points which were debated and the conclusions which were reached.

PRIMARY OBJECTIVE

Most important of all was the discussion on the formulation of the company's primary objective in the first section of the document, since the concept of social resources and the idea of interdependent and complementary economic and social objectives lent cohesion to the whole of the rest of the statement.

The concept of social resources itself and the notion that the company had only legal rights of privileged access to its resources rather than owning them absolutely was different from the traditional concept of property. Also unfamiliar was to think of employees as being social resources to be protected and developed, rather than "commodities," however well they might be treated. Yet the concept was accepted without much argument. Whilst the idea came initially as a shock, the oil industry is sufficiently familar with practical examples of the right of access to resources being withdrawn from companies by some societies through nationalisation or expropriation, for the concept to be recognised as relevant. Most of those present had worked in many parts of the world and between them had a fund of experience in dealing with the problems of setting up a new refinery—finding and recruiting people from the local communities and training them before the start-up so they could run it. It was not difficult to perceive such people as social resources.

There was, however, strong argument about the use of the term "profitability" in preference to "profits." The latter represented finite sums of money, the former a state of affairs which had continuously to be maintained, if the enterprise was to survive. A vast concern like Shell was in business "for keeps." It was not expendable and it was intimately involved in many critical ways with the societies in which it operated. That it should continue to succeed and how it used its power were both important issues to many people beyond itself.

The main debate concerned the validity of extending the scope of the primary objective beyond the commitment to maximise contributions to the group's long-term profitability. It was considered by some that the inclusion of the words "long-term" automatically ruled out any undesirable or anti-social methods of making profits, since such activity would inevitably have adverse repercussions on the company's reputation and its long-term prospects. In response to this argument it was agreed that senior managers would tend to carry in their minds to varying degrees the complex implications attaching to the phrase "long-term profitability." They were relatively well equipped from their privileged position in the company to be able to commit themselves to work towards such a complex overall objective. It was unlikely, however, that the man on the shop floor would carry a similar set of implications in his mind. His set of implications would tend to be quite different, particularly if he—and others—interpreted the word "profitability" to mean simply the profits distributed annually to shareholders, the

F

dividends always being made as large as possible at his expense. What the company was now seeking was an overall objective which all employees in the organisation could understand in the same way and to which they could all commit themselves. It was therefore essential to spell out exactly what it should be and not to rely on implications which could differ between individuals, or might not be recognised at all.

In order to focus the argument, it was suggested there were three possible formulations of the primary objective the drafters could have used: they were referred to as position 1, position 2, and position 3, the latter corresponding to the formulation used in the statement although for the purpose of this explication, it was put in a simpler form. They were:

Position 1. The company is primarily concerned to maximise its contribution to the long-term profitability of the Group.

Position 2. The company is primarily concerned to maximise its contribution to the long-term profitability of the Group, with due regard for its social obligations for the welfare of its employees and the community.

Position 3. The company is primarily concerned to maximise its contribution to the long-term profitability of the Group insofar as this arises from the efficiency with which it uses the Group's resources of men, money and material, accepting that these are social resources to be used for meeting society's requirements.

Position 1

It was argued that position 1 represents profit maximisation without any qualification. It corresponded to the objectives which had been drafted by the top management team after their meeting in March 1965, of which the primary objective was: "to maximise the return on capital employed for the company, having due regard for manufacturing costs." This may be the conventional way of stating the objective of a business but an individual working in an organisation strictly guided by such a primary objective would tend to adopt a similar self-seeking attitude and would strive simply to maximise his own personal gain. Unions would see no reason why they should not struggle to get the biggest possible share of the cake. If profit maximisation was the rule of the game, it was their job to learn to play it was well as they could. The example was quoted of the explicit adoption of just such a philosophy by unions in the United States after the Second World War (in place of the class struggle), and this had now crossed the Atlantic. Such a philosophy also told managers that their primary objective was their own career interests. To be over-concerned about the good of the company was irrational.

Position 2

Position 2 recognised that the company has some social obligations which are seen as constraints on profit maximisation. Whilst legal constraints are normally observed, and whilst the company may choose on occasion to go beyond legal requirements, it reserves the right to cut back whenever it feels it necessary to do so. Thus the choice as to the degree of social obligation which should be recognised in any particular situation is left entirely up to the company which retains complete control in its own hands. Employees in an organisation guided by a position 2 objective would be unlikely to trust the management always to exercise its discretion in a fair and consistent manner. They may see it as a technique to buy off individual self-seeking. Such distrust would be confirmed and strengthened if the company chose to revert to position 1 in hard times, which position 2 leaves it free to do. At such times, paternalism would be replaced by the hard line. Employees would find their suspicions justified and would become angry and cynical. The way the recent reductions in manning levels had been carried out had led to serious repercussions and had caused a marked degree of alienation within the ranks of management itself.

Position 3

Position 3 differs from 2 in that it builds in an amalgamation of economic and social values and a criterion for their reconciliation: the commitment to efficient use of social resources. It openly commits the company to observe the amalgamation. It does not allow a reversion to position 1. It lays the foundations for company objectives to which it would be hoped the commitment of all employees could in the long run be secured and an attitude of trust built up.

During the discussion there was some initial support from a few of the managers present for the position 1 approach. Although they agreed the company did not operate in that way, they were reluctant to commit to paper any constraints on profit maximisation (beyond those implied by "long-term") when they had no clear and rational criteria for doing so. It was generally felt that in the past the company's position had been that described in position 2. It was recognised, however, that there had on occasions been swings back to position 1, with apparent disregard of social obligations and that this oscillation between 2 and 1 had undoubtedly contributed a great deal to the high level of distrust of management's intentions, not only among shop-floor employees but also among supervisors and managers. A simpler example of such oscillation than the manner of the 1964 rundown, was the extension of facilities for part-time studies enjoyed by staff workers to the hourly paid employees in the early 1960s and the subsequent withdrawal of these facilities a year or two later. Such pinpricks not only annoyed; they were symbolic.

It was finally agreed by everyone that position 3 most appropriately described what the company was now setting out to do. It was particularly necessary to move in this direction in view of the accelerating rate of technological change and the higher level of uncertainty this brought about for all. Position 3 offered the prospect of establishing a positive and consistent pattern of management, a stable anchor in an unstable world. The conjunction of the economic objective and the social objective was felt to be valid and acceptable. Moreover, it was considered that far from being a constraint on profitability, the recognition of the need to protect and develop social resources would in the long term prove to be contributing to the company's profitability. To treat employees as resources and to develop their talents would be more than ever necessary in the more automated and changing world of the future. The two parts of the primary objective were not opposed but complementary.

Implications of position 3

Some of the implications of accepting position 3 as the primary objective were explored in depth. For example, it meant that profit could be sought only through the efficient use of resources: profit from exploitation or degrading of resources would be contrary to the objective. This applied equally to the treatment of people, raw material, equipment, money or the environment. It ruled out such activities as the crude use of market power, or price fixing, as a substitute for the continuing search for improved competence in the manufacture of competitive products of quality. By committing themselves explicitly to this social objective of protecting and developing its resources, managers would be open to question by employees if their decisions appeared to be inconsistent with it. Further, in establishing social objectives down the line, alongside operational objectives, as would have to be done, it would become necessary to give greater recognition to social costs than had been done in the past, whether these were borne by employees (for example, in terms of stress or obsolescence), or by the community (in terms of nuisance or pollution).

Clearly, however, some limits had to be set. The commitment to protect and develop resources could not be open-ended. The principle was accordingly established that the commitment should apply only to those resources which the company used. It was not committing itself to expenditure on community resources which it did not itself use. Further, the level to which it should protect and develop its resources was to be interpreted in accordance with the prevailing standards and values of society.

To take a practical example, the company could not unilaterally be committed to eliminate all pollution resulting from its operations regardless of the cost. Yet some managers felt the company should undertake some measure of leadership in this respect. Taking a leadership role meant anticipating the future: it meant seeking improved solutions by setting its own reasonable example and by using its influence to secure the co-operation of others. The result of this discussion, and of similar discussions with groups of managers at the refineries, was to build a guide-line into the document by the addition of the phrase "accepting the measures practised under comparable conditions in British industry as a minimum standard" to specific objective 2:6 which then read: "seeking to reduce any interference that may be caused by its activities to the amenities of the community, accepting the measures practised under comparable conditions in British industry as a minimum standard and making use of the expertise and knowledge available within the Group."

The company's position within the Group

Discussion of the third paragraph of section 1 of the statement, which describes the implications of the company's relationships with the Group, served to reinforce several already recognised needs. Separated from the market at both the crude input and the product output ends, the company had no meaningful profit indicators by which to measure its own efficiency. In their early visits to the refineries, the Tavistock team had found this to be a cause of great anxiety among manufacturing people, allied with feelings of inferiority to and resentment of marketing people. It encouraged misleading beliefs about profit centres in manufacturing locations, beliefs which were particularly unsuited to Group balancing refineries. The company's specific objectives had therefore to be framed in terms of meeting the requirements put upon it with the minimum expenditure of resources. This did not equate with cost-cutting. It meant meeting market requirements in a way which "used up" the minimum of its total resources and which was compatible with protecting and developing its resources.

Discussion of the implications of this situation led to the underlining of the need for the company to generate more effective yardsticks of its own performance. Also underlined was the need for better communication channels across the company boundary with the Group central supply unit and with the marketing organisation. This would permit more information to flow into the company and provide greater opportunity for the company to challenge decisions affecting its operations. As the potential benefits this would bring were perceived at company level, so it was recognised that people at the refineries would have similar needs and similar potential benefits at their level.

As one result of this debate, which was to be enlarged upon at refinery conferences, a new specific objective 2 : 3, was in due course added to the statement. It had not appeared in the original draft. It read: "In addition, the company is specifically committed to: seeking continually from the Group the power and information necessary to enable it to meet its responsibilities. In certain circumstances it may be necessary to seek a redefinition of its responsibilities in order that the company's capabilities may be best used on behalf of the Group."

JOINT OPTIMISATION AS A GUIDE TO IMPLEMENTATION

The initial difficulty with this section of the statement was caused partly by the terminology but also partly by the newness of the concept itself.

Whilst it was conceded that the use of jargon should be minimised, the terminology of the statement was defended by Tavistock on the grounds that every branch of knowledge has its own set of concepts which people have to learn if they want to understand what it has to offer. Furthermore, an advantage of the use of the appropriate terminology was that it ensured that important points would be adequately discussed and explored. A danger inherent in the use of paraphrase was that people would tend to accept points as obvious, without considering their implications. Thus while "joint optimisation of the socio-technical system" at first gave people pause and demanded explanations a paraphrase such as "the best matching of the people and the equipment in the organisation" might be accepted as reasonable or self-evident and passed over without challenge.

The conference members in this case accepted without difficulty the notion that any production system consists of two parts: the social system, made up of people, with their physical and psychological requirements and characteristics, and the way they are organised, both formally and informally, in the work situation; and the technical system, comprising the equipment and plant with its particular characteristics and requirements and the way it is laid out. The idea of joint optimisation was that these two sub-systems should be matched together in the most appropriate and effective way.

The main difficulty shared, however, by most managers was to imagine that there could be any better or significantly different way of organising people to operate a process unit, or any other piece of equipment, than the traditional way in which it had always been done. Until it was accepted that there was in fact a wide range of choice in the way the social and the technical systems could be matched together, the real significance of the concept of joint optimisation was not apparent. What served to bring home to the conference members the meaning of organisational choice was a graphic description by one of the Tavistock team of the contrast in effectiveness between the two methods of operating the Longwall coal faces (the conventional and the composite), already referred to in Chapter 3. From this point on, the possibility of applying the concept within the refinery situation became more real.

The socio-technical approach to designing jobs and organisations was seen as striking a balance, in a sense, between the two main theories which had previously governed—and mostly still do govern—the way jobs are set up.

The most common approach to job-design has always been machine-dominated. This is the mechanistic or "scientific management" approach (F W Taylor, 1911), which regards the people who must operate equipment virtually as extensions of the machinery. In other words, their distinctive human capabilities and needs are not taken into account, and their jobs are closely specified, almost as if the people themselves were mechanically controlled. Thus the maximum degree of break-down or specialisation of tasks is sought, leading to a high level of repetitive work and a minimum need for training of people to learn the job. A strong supervisory system is supplied in an effort to make sure people do not depart from the prescribed tasks. The basis for motivation of people in this approach is seen as purely economic, to be secured by appropriate financial rewards.

Time and motion study, payment by results schemes, and much of current industrial engineering have derived from this traditional mechanistic approach to job design. In a situation where the work force is willing to submit to boring, tiring, repetitive jobs, the approach clearly produces results. In a situation, however, where the work force becomes frustrated and antagonised by the nature of their tasks, the system can easily be disrupted if they behave in ways other than those laid down.

If the scientific management approach concerns itself mainly with the technical system, the second major approach—the human relations school—is concerned almost entirely with the social system. The human relations school sprang from the work of Elton Mayo who, through his studies at the Hawthorne works of the Western Electric Company over the years 1927–33, demonstrated that the social system in an organisation had very distinctive characteristics of its own (Roethlisberger & Dickson 1939). These and other subsequent studies have shown how the morale of a group is affected by the quality of inter-personal relationships within the group, and between the group and its supervisor. They identified the informal groups which exist alongside the formal and showed how the commitment of a group to a common objective provided a motivational force which could overcome the effects of unfavourable changes in physical working conditions.

The human relations approach with its stress on the attitude of the individual, his role in his group and his status in the social system, undoubtedly led to improvements in working conditions, welfare arrangements and employee services. It also encouraged the employment of personnel counsellors, to help employees resolve their psychological problems. But it was focused exclusively on the social system with virtually no regard to the effect the technical system had upon people's actual tasks. Its usefulness has accordingly tended to be limited.

The essentially new feature of Tavistock's socio-technical approach to job design was the recognition that because of their interdependence, the social and the technical systems had to be considered together. As the coal mine studies had clearly demonstrated, it was necessary to analyse exactly what requirements the technical system imposed upon the people who operated it: only then was it possible to organise the tasks in a way which both satisfied the technical requirements and made the best use of the properties of the social system itself. Interestingly, these properties were the exact opposite to the demands made upon people in an organisation designed on scientific management lines.

The scientific management approach required people to carry out simple repetitive tasks in a consistent manner over long periods of time: machines are eminently suited to this type of task; people are not. The socio-technical approach, by contrast, seeks to utilise those capabilities of the social system which are distinctively human: for example, the ability to be flexible, and adaptive, to make judgements and take decisions. Only by matching these human capabilities with the complementary characteristics of the technology could the best overall result be obtained.

Furthermore, by arranging tasks in a way which enables people to utilise their distinctive capabilities, the socio-technical approach opens up the possibility of motivating people through their interest in and commitment to their work, rather than simply through financial rewards as in the scientific management approach.

That people should be interested in and committed to their work becomes particularly necessary in advanced and changing technologies. The statement's examination of the key characteristics of the company's refining technology brought out the fact that the basic skills required were perceptual and cognitive. People had to use good judgement and make good decisions: this could not be secured by external supervision. Hence the importance of involvement and commitment. To correct errors after they had occurred was too late and too costly. Men had to be self-regulating and internally motivated to anticipate events. This was not simply desirable, it was essential for the efficient operation of the system.

Practical implications
The outcome of this discussion was general agreement that the concept of joint optimisation was highly relevant to the company's situation. Furthermore, the technical managers present said it was clear that in the past, the company had concentrated very much on optimising the technical system. Only after the design of a new technical system was completed would the question of manning it normally be considered. The concept of joint optimisation clearly implied the need to plan technical and social systems together if the best results were to be achieved. The new refinery at Teesport provided an opportunity to do this and how it was tackled is described in Chapter 13.

Another major implication of acceptance of this concept—and one which was to be discussed again at many location conferences—was that the manager of a department must be responsible for the entire socio-technical system and not only for meeting his operational targets. The tendency in the past had often been for the manager to concentrate his attention on the problems of the technical system and to pass problems arising in the social system to the personnel department to deal with.

PSYCHOLOGICAL NEEDS

Section 6 of the document, dealing with the conditions which have to be provided if people are to develop responsibility and commitment to their tasks, was accepted by the management team as relevant to the refinery situation. There was general agreement that in many parts of the organisation, the company was not fully utilising its human capabilities. There were also doubts, however, about the extent to which it would be possible in practice to establish appropriate conditions for some sections of the work force, but there again the limits of what might be feasible were not known.

RESULTS OF THE CONFERENCE

During the concluding session on the third day of the conference, at Tavistock's suggestion, each manager present gave his personal reactions to the contents of the draft statement. The managing director reserved his own views until last.

The outcome was that each manager accepted the document as valid and appropriate to the company's needs. Each gave his commitment to manage in accordance with its principles. It was felt that it contained objectives from which a positive and stable philosophy of management had been derived and offered the means of releasing unused human capabilities and of improving motivation and commitment. The level of enthusiasm varied and some reservations were expressed but overall there was strong support for the statement. One manager considered this event could well prove to be the most important management conference the company had ever held. The managing director made clear his own support of the principles and said that the three days' test-out of the document had dispelled some initial scepticism. He then stated his personal commitment.

The reservations expressed were concerned mainly with the difficulty foreseen in getting the statement widely disseminated and understood throughout the company and uncertainty, at this stage, about how the ideas in the philosophy could be put into practice. Conference members themselves would need more time to consider fully the implications of the document for their own roles and their own departments. It was also felt necessary to see how senior managers in the refineries reacted to the philosophy before it was transmitted down the line, and certainly before the trade unions were involved in any way.

Action items
The following decisions were taken before the conference was wound up:
1 In view of the successful outcome of the trial period, and the acceptance of the draft statement, the action research relationship with Tavistock would be extended, so that they could help with the dissemination process and with the development of the programme. It was recognised that their participation in the Selsdon Park conference had been a critical factor in its success.
2 Each refinery, and head office, would hold their own conferences to discuss the statement with their own senior staff. Tavistock and ERP would be available to help, if requested.
3 When all senior staff in the company had had the opportunity to work through the document, a further conference of the management team would be held early in 1966 to review progress, and decide what further steps to take.
4 The statement of objectives and philosophy would continue to be regarded as a draft. It was anticipated that additional modifications and improvements would be proposed from staff at the refineries. ERP was to be the custodian of the draft, responsible for collecting and co-ordinating all suggested amendments to the text.
5 Until the statement had proved acceptable to refinery senior staff and the programme was more firmly established, it should be given the minimum publicity necessary to avoid undesirable rumours. It was suggested that at the refineries, where the absence at conferences of numbers of senior staff could hardly go unnoticed, it should be stated simply that the company was studying in depth its objectives and method of operating, and that if and when there was anything further to communicate, it would be done.
6 Location managements should begin to consider what were the implications of the statement within their commands, in terms of action to be taken, both at their own level and at less-senior levels in the organisation.

Chapter 8

Debating the Statement Down the Line

Following the acceptance of the draft statement by the company top management team at Selsdon Park, the next step was to seek similar acceptance from people down the line. What was envisaged was a cascade of conferences at each location, spreading down eventually to the shop floor. At these conferences, all participants would have the same opportunity as the top management to debate and test out the contents of the document against their own experience and to explore its implications. They would be free to accept it or reject it for themselves.

The dissemination programme was something entirely new in the company. Nothing like it had been attempted before. Moreover, there was no blue-print laying down how the process was to be organised or conducted. Each location manager was responsible for running his own programme in the way he felt would best suit the requirements of his situation.

The role of Tavistock and ERP was to assist the location managers to achieve this. The Tavistock team had wide experience and skills in helping to secure frank and open debate of issues in a conference situation. ERP, who continued to work in close collaboration with Tavistock, were available to assist with the planning and organisation of conferences and to record and co-ordinate events, keeping managers informed of developments on a company-wide basis.

This chapter will describe the dissemination process under the following headings:

Phase 1—senior staff

Management conference to review progress
Phase 2—other staff and shop floor
Effects of the process

The involvement of trade union officials and of shop stewards in the process will be covered in Chapter 9.

PHASE 1—SENIOR STAFF

A total of about 270 senior staff across the company were involved in phase 1. Refinery general managers had been asked to complete their conference programmes for these people before the progress review took place in early 1966. The outcome of this phase was also critical for the future of the overall development programme. Without the support of the influential layer of managers involved, it would clearly not be feasible to continue.

Although locations were to adopt significantly different patterns of dissemination, there were certain features which they all shared. For example, each refinery manager invited members of the Tavistock and ERP teams to help plan his conference programme and to sit in as advisers at the conference events.

A planning meeting was held at each refinery before the first conference took place. Decisions were taken on such matters as:

1 *Pre-reading material*—this was kept to a minimum, but included the draft statement and usually an introductory book on applied social science: Ed Schein's (1965) "Organisational Psychology" was most frequently used.

2 *Membership*—about twenty people were normally invited to attend. A system of overlapping membership was followed, so that each new conference was also attended by a few people who had already attended a previous event. They provided continuity and could, as additional resources, help forward the process of discussion. This experience consolidated their own understanding and equipped them for the role of discussion leaders at the phase 2 conferences.

3 *Place*—away from the site, usually in a hotel with conference centre facilities, under residential conditions and protected from interruption.

4 *Timing*—many of the phase 1 conferences took place over the weekend; later ones were scheduled for mid-week, to emphasise that they constituted relevant and legitimate work. Programmes were planned to

take an evening and two days, a day less than the Selsdon Park conference.

5 *Objectives*—the basic objective was to secure a full understanding of the contents of the draft statement and to seek people's commitment to it. An added objective at later conferences, as experience was gained in achieving the first objective faster, was to explore ways of disseminating the philosophy further down the line and ways of putting it into effect.

6 *Agenda*—a broad framework was agreed but exact time allocation was left flexible, so that it could respond to the actual pace of progress through the document.

Each of the phase 1 conferences was chaired by the refinery general manager, or his deputy. Apart from explaining the background to the conference, however, they did not attempt to feed in the points of debate which had arisen at Selsdon Park. The conference members were accordingly encouraged to react spontaneously to the document and to be open and frank in their discussion.

Within this common framework, the different patterns which emerged are described below.

Stanlow

After Selsdon Park, the general manager at Stanlow and his deputy were keen to get their own conference programme started. They seemed confident that the statement would be acceptable to their senior staff and would be seen as relevant to the refinery situation. They were the first to mount a location conference. Even with one day less available than at Selsdon Park, they hoped to be able to get through the contents of the statement and use some time at the end for consideration of its implications for Stanlow.

People at the first conference were very much concerned with the same issues which had taken up the time at Selsdon Park. Argument was serious and intense and continued on an informal basis until late into the night. Discussion of the company's primary and specific objectives, for example, was particularly vigorous. Clearly Stanlow's own objectives had to be consistent with them and this focussed attention on the fact that many people at Stanlow tended to operate as if the refinery objective was to maximise its own profitability, rather than to contribute to that of the company, and thus to the Group. It also led to a strong claim for a specific objective to be added which would make explicit the refinery's right to challenge any head office decisions which would, out of ignorance of local conditions, impose greater expenditure of resources than was necessary to meet its product targets. This reaction was similar to the one already reported at Selsdon Park, but arose quite independently.

There was also spontaneous recognition that in the past much attention had been given at the refinery to solving technological and economic problems, but considerably less to the problems of the social system, in terms other than fire-fighting. The need for a programme which would do something to improve motivation and performance was therefore strongly endorsed.

The approach adopted by Stanlow management to the further three conferences in phase 1 was essentially dynamic. Improvements or additions to the draft statement suggested at one conference were fed into the next one. Recommendations made by conference members for making better use of the time available were tried out during the next event. The result was a visible process of development, towards which the conference members were clearly contributing. By the forth and last conference of phase 1, the working through of the document was taking place in two sub-groups, which meant that progress was faster and that much more time was available for considering implementation possibilities.

The design for the fourth conference is shown in Figure 8:1. It will be seen that by the end of the first full day, the contents of the draft statement had been worked through and the two sub-groups had reported their reactions to each other. The whole of the next day was spent first on generating ideas about implementation in four small sub-groups and then discussing them as a full group. An advantage of this design was that whilst the four sub-groups were meeting on their own in the morning, the management and the Tavistock and ERP people were able to meet separately as a planning group to decide on future strategy and developments.

Shell Haven

The management approach at Shell Haven was quite different from Stanlow's. They wanted to move more slowly and not to rush into their first conference. Confronted by a long-standing industrial relations problem at the refinery, and a relatively poor level of morale, they wanted to be sure their senior staff were committed to the contents of the draft statement before time was spent considering implementation possibili-

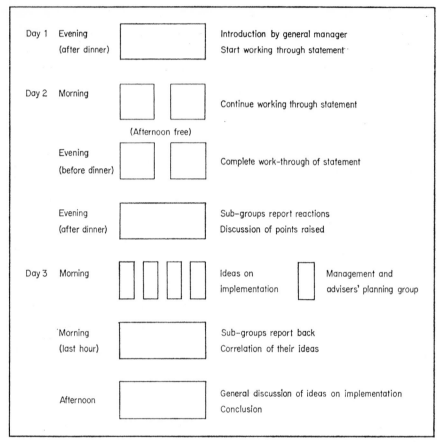

Day 1	Evening (after dinner)		Introduction by general manager Start working through statement
Day 2	Morning		Continue working through statement
	(Afternoon free)		
	Evening (before dinner)		Complete work-through of statement
	Evening (after dinner)		Sub-groups report reactions Discussion of points raised
Day 3	Morning		Ideas on implementation — Management and advisers' planning group
	Morning (last hour)		Sub-groups report back Correlation of their ideas
	Afternoon		General discussion of ideas on implementation Conclusion

FIGURE 8:1 DESIGN FOR A STANLOW PHASE 1 DISSEMINATION
CONFERENCE

ties. Accordingly key people among the senior staff were briefed before
the first conference and when it took place the whole of the time was
scheduled for working through the statement. Unlike Stanlow, no time
was allowed during the first phase conferences for a study of implementation ideas, nor was the membership broken down into sub-groups.

As the refinery general manager and his deputy had anticipated,
much of the time at the first conference was taken up with the problem
of morale. It seemed that some of the members needed to convince
themselves that the management of the company really intended to
put the new philosophy into practice, before they could be happy about
disseminating it further down the line. These doubts sprang from the
oscillations of management styles in previous years, and were given
point by the run-down in numbers in 1964 which, particularly at Shell

Haven, had upset a number of people through the mode of its introduction. Anxiety was also expressed about the future of the refinery.

These matters were discussed in the course of working through the document in terms of whether, if the philosophy had then been in force, things would have been handled differently. This did not detract from the general acceptance of the statement, nor did it prevent a number of suggestions being made for amendments and improvements.

Unlike Stanlow, however, such proposals for amending the document, although recorded, were not passed on to subsequent conferences. People attending all three conferences in phase 1 were given the same draft document and followed an identical programme. The general principle was that everyone attending a conference would be exposed to exactly the same treatment. In this way, when the process moved further down the line any suspicions that some people were receiving special or biased treatment could be shown to be unfounded.

Head office

The head office conferences were handled differently from both major refineries. They were held in the company's main office, on a non-residential basis. They therefore lacked two of the principal advantages of the off-site events run by the refineries. First, the advantage of being away from the normal place of work and its inevitable interruptions, which undoubtedly made it easier for the refinery staff to stand back, as it were, from their normal routines, and take a fresh look at what the company was trying to do and how it was managing its affairs. Secondly, except for an evening buffet session, they lacked the opportunity for the sort of extended informal discussion at the end of the day's formal programme which had proved so valuable at some refinery conferences, particularly at Stanlow.

Head office staff also faced more complex problems than refinery staff. The role of the head office was less well defined. The different departments or functions were less well integrated than at the refineries. At the refineries the interdepartmental membership of the conferences made sense, since all the departments were sufficiently closely interlinked to be able usefully to discuss together the implications of the philosophy statement. At head office, however, it became apparent that some departments worked almost in isolation from others and would not gain much from sharing discussion of implications or implementation measures with them.

After the initial working through of the draft statement with the

G

senior people, therefore, it was decided that each function should hold its own separate departmental meetings to consider with its own staff what the statement implied for its role and its method of operation. In examining their own roles, head office departments were particularly concerned with specific objective 2:2 of the draft statement: "ensuring the company's ability to meet emerging market requirements with decreasing expenditure of total resources per unit of quantity of specified quality."

This implied for them a special role of leadership in the organisation and a capability for innovation and creativity, rather than the capacity to serve merely as a post office and a co-ordinating body.

The functional meetings led to a number of action items being listed and pursued. Perhaps the most important were the steps taken to strengthen existing communication channels with appropriate units in the Group, and with the marketing organisation, so that the company could not only get better information but could also exert greater influence. Another important outcome was the recognition of the need to involve the refineries more, for example, in operations planning activities carried out in head office, a need which had also been expressed quite strongly at some refinery conferences.

Briefing of Group
Whilst the phase 1 conferences were in progress, the managing director was also concerned with advising the appropriate people in the Group, both in London and The Hague, about the development programme and its aims. Other Shell companies in the UK were similarly informed. As the result of a briefing session with the top management team of Shell Chemical Company Limited, the previous decision that the two chemical plants based at the major refineries would participate in the programme was confirmed. Shell Chemical Company management decided, however, that it would not be appropriate for the rest of their organisation, which included UK marketing, to involve itself. They were themselves studying other routes to improving performance.

The general reaction to the briefing sessions, which usually lasted a day, was one of great interest and support. To some of the technical people, the programme seemed a little elaborate and sophisticated. There was, however, endorsement of the values embodied in the statement, and an assurance that the company's commitment to manage its resources in a manner which would protect and develop them, was consistent with the way the Group considered operating companies should conduct their affairs and their relationships with the communities in which they operated.

When the location conferences got further down the line, considerable concern was often expressed about how the programme would be viewed by the Group. If location managements had not been able to give an account of the extensive activities of the managing director in securing the sympathetic support of people at Group central offices, credibility would have been lost.

MANAGEMENT CONFERENCE TO REVIEW PROGRESS

The conference to review progress was held in March 1966. It took place again at Selsdon Park and the membership was essentially the same as at the original October 1965 conference, with a few additional management representatives, including the deputy managing director, who had recently joined the company from overseas, and the head of the training department. The purpose of the conference was to take stock of what the programme had achieved so far, to confirm the commitment of the managers to its continuance, and to take decisions on future courses of action.

In opening the conference, the managing director explained the steps he had taken to tell senior people in the Group about the development programme. He assured the members that there was Group support for what the company was trying to do and that there was great interest to see in due course what changes could be brought about as a result of the implementation of the philosophy.

The main outcomes of the conference are summarised below:

1 The draft statement. A redrafted version of the statement, which incorporated many of the suggestions for additions and improvements made at the phase 1 conferences, was accepted by everyone present as representing the best text to date. It was agreed that it was now unlikely that any further significant amendments would be put forward and that the draft should be frozen in its present form for the next twelve months. It is this frozen version which appears in Chapter 6, and which in fact was to remain unchanged from 1966 onwards.

It was also agreed that it would be useful if Tavistock and ERP produced a written commentary on the statement, which would include some elucidation of those parts of the draft which had caused most debate during the phase 1 conferences. It was thought that the commentary would be of great help to anyone leading a group through a discussion of the meaning and implications of the draft statement. The commentary is reproduced in Appendix 3.

2 *Further dissemination of the philosophy.* The refinery managers expressed some doubts about the extent to which some of the senior staff who had taken part in conferences so far had fully understood the statement and its implications. It was agreed, however, that a significant number of senior staff were now committed to the philosophy and a much larger number knew that the company management was committed and intended to go ahead with implementation measures. In the opinion of the Tavistock advisers, the phase 1 conferences had achieved their objectives and there was now undoubtedly a "critical mass" of committed people which would enable the dissemination process to be carried forward.

It was therefore agreed that the dissemination of the philosophy would be carried on down the line to foreman level and subsequently to the hourly paid employees. The timing and method of the process would again be left to the refinery managers. It was the general view, however, that all conferences should continue to be run by line managers and that, in view of the large number of people to be covered, this task would have to be spread fairly widely among senior staff at the refineries. It was thought useful to continue the pattern of basing conference membership on mixed groups of staff from different departments and it was suggested that as the process involved people lower down the line, some simplified version of the statement would prove helpful. Tavistock and ERP undertook to work on this. The idea of a simplified version tied in with the assumption that people down the line would be less concerned with the content and format of the document and more concerned with its practical implications for them in their own job situations.

There was a strong feeling, particularly from the Stanlow representatives, that in parallel with the second phase of dissemination conferences, there should be some visible signs of implementation. They felt it was essential to demonstrate to all employees that management intended to put the philosophy into practice and to show how this could be done. They were also concerned that enthusiasm generated by the conferences would turn to disillusion if practical measures were delayed too long.

3 *Involvement of the trade unions.* It was agreed that the trade union officials and the shop stewards would need to be involved in the next

phase of the dissemination process. This would have to take place before a start could be made on any implementation measures which would affect trade union members and where their collaboration would accordingly be necessary.

Discussion with union officials at national level was envisaged, with the participation of Tavistock members. Refineries would also make direct approaches to their own local officials and shop stewards when they judged the time was appropriate.

4 *Implementation measures.* A review showed a considerable number of areas where the philosophy had already affected management decisions or led to changes in attitude. One example was the decision to set up a small team to review the role of the refinery personnel department and its relationships with line departments in the light of the implications of the philosophy statement. It was envisaged that with line managers assuming more responsibility for their own social systems, the personnel department would be able to do more forward planning and less daily fire-fighting.

A number of further specific action proposals were agreed:

(*a*) *Pilot projects.* Some sites would be selected where the principle of joint optimisation could be tried out on an experimental basis. As the projects would involve hourly paid employees, and possibly changes in their jobs, the agreement of the trade unions and shop stewards would be needed before a start could be made. A description of these pilot projects, which in the event were all located at Stanlow, is given in Chapter 11.

(*b*) *Joint working parties.* Special working parties would be set up at the refineries to prepare proposals on which productivity bargains could be based. They would be made up of representatives from management and from the shop floor but their terms of reference would be quite different from those which normally applied to any such groups involved in the process of productivity bargaining. Their task would be to develop, in a non-bargaining frame of reference, a set of terms and conditions of employment for shop-floor work people which they could jointly recommend to the unions and to the management. At that stage, their proposals would be fed into the normal bargaining machinery.

It was considered essential that before such working parties could be established, their purpose should be made clear to the trade union officials and shop stewards and their agreement obtained. This action item also depended, therefore, on a successful discussion with trade union representatives about the philosophy programme. An account of the work of the joint working parties, and what they achieved, is given in Chapter 14.

(c) *Bargaining machinery.* Head office would attempt to persuade the TGWU to agree to the decentralisation of the existing national agreement which covered the three refineries at Stanlow, Shell Haven and Ardrossan. This would enable separate locally negotiated agreements to be set up in its place, so that each refinery could proceed at its own pace with the productivity bargaining which it was hoped would stem from the results of the joint working parties.

(d) *Refinery objectives.* Refinery general managers would begin the process of defining their own and their immediate subordinates' responsibilities and role relationships, as a start to the task of producing a hierarchy of consistent objectives at department and unit levels within the refineries. Shell Haven management had already made some progress on this task.

(e) *Training.* Refineries would attempt to arrange some external courses for their supervisory staff and shop stewards at which they could gain some familiarity with management theory and with the social sciences. Stanlow had already arranged such a programme at a local training college.

PHASE 2: OTHER STAFF AND SHOP FLOOR

After the review meeting in March 1966, a second wave of conferences was embarked upon throughout the company, except at head office where, in view of the follow-up meetings which had taken place in each department, no more formal conferences took place. All locations found it possible to work through the draft statement more quickly and to spend more time on considering implementation possibilities. This was partly because the managers who guided the discussions were becoming more familiar with the statement and more skilled at leading the group through it but also because, as had been anticipated, the people lower down the line were less concerned to argue about the concepts in the document than their more senior colleagues had been.

At differing times, the two major refineries decided to discontinue formal conferences and to disseminate the philosophy to the remainder of the work force who had not participated in one by means of departmental discussion groups, led by the department managers. For this purpose, the simplified version of the statement produced by Tavistock and ERP proved useful and it was also used at some of the later formal conferences. The text is quoted in Appendix 4.

As a result of these changes, refineries requested a considerably reduced level of support at their conferences from Tavistock and ERP. Whereas at the initial phase 1 conferences there were normally at least two people from Tavistock and two from ERP present, support was now reduced to one from each team or less. This was helpful, since it allowed them more time to assist with the development of implementation measures.

An added and valuable source of assistance during this period was the participation in the programme of a number of overseas social scientists. These were mainly people who were taking sabbatical leave from their own institutions and were basing themselves on Tavistock in London. They included: Dr Godfrey Gardener, University of Melbourne; Professor Stanley Seashore, University of Michigan; Professor Martin Lakin, Duke University, North Carolina; and Professor Louis Davis, University of California, Los Angeles.

These visitors, who were not all in the UK at the same time, participated in the planning meetings which Tavistock and ERP regularly held and took the place of the Tavistock representative at many of the second wave philosophy conferences. In addition, Lou Davis assisted with one of the pilot projects at Stanlow dealing with the interface between engineering maintenance and process operations.

Because of their own wide experience in the field of organisation development, these overseas collaborators were able to make a valuable contribution to the company's programme. Furthermore, they were able to look critically at the whole approach from close quarters and it was noteworthy that they were without exception impressed with its scope and originality.

There were also changes in the membership of the Tavistock team during this period. Eric Trist, who had led the original team, left the UK at the end of 1966, and whilst remaining a part-time member of the Institute, took up an appointment at the University of California, Los Angeles, where he joined Lou Davis to develop the first graduate programme in socio-technical studies attempted in a university. Later he joined Russell Ackoff at the Management and Behavioural Science Center at the University of Pennsylvania, to develop the interface between OR and the behavioural sciences, which Ackoff had helped the Tavistock to develop in the UK. Fred Emery took over the team leadership but was himself to leave the UK in September 1967 for a year's stay at the Center for Advanced Study in the Behavioral Sciences at Stanford. He then returned to Australia where, from a base in the Research School in Social Sciences at the Australian National University, Canberra, he has developed a research programme which includes socio-technical and other work in collaboration with Hollis Peter, adviser to the Shell Company in Australia, to which some of the managers involved in the Shell UK programme have gone. Meanwhile, Hans van Beinum joined the team and was mainly concerned with the pilot projects at Stanlow, being responsible for their overall direction. He has since taken up a chair in organisation behaviour at the new Business School in Rotterdam and also advises Shell in The Hague. Michael Foster, another Tavistock member, was closely involved in the development with ERP of simplified methods of socio-technical analysis (described in Chapter 12) and later became the main source of Tavistock assistance.

Some aspects of the phase 2 conferences at the two major refineries are described below.

Stanlow

Between April and September 1966, Stanlow ran a series of twenty-seven residential conferences for mixed groups of staff including foremen and supervisors. They also ran, during June and July, a conference for local trade union officials and two conferences for their senior shop stewards. These last three events are described in Chapter 9.

About half-way through the series, on the basis of the experience gained, the design of the conferences was changed. It was decided to spend only one day and one evening on working through the statement in the off-site hotel and to cover the discussion of implementation items at departmental meetings held subsequently at the refinery.

After the series ended in September, dissemination to junior staff and to the hourly paid employees was all handled through departmental discussion groups. Four intensive seminars for department managers were held at Stanlow with Tavistock and ERP present to help them develop ideas on how this task could best be handled. The departmental discussion groups were also seen as an important channel for generating implementation measures and they will be mentioned again in this context in Chapter 12.

These variations in the Stanlow dissemination programme provide an interesting example of the way in which conference members were involved in making decisions which would affect the future of the programme. As already described, Stanlow management wanted to get the union officials and the shop stewards involved in the programme so that a start could be made on setting up pilot projects and establishing the joint working parties. This meant that an approach would have to be made to them long before all the supervisory staff had had an opportunity to attend a dissemination conference. The risk of offending the supervisory staff group was accordingly high.

In order to avoid this, Stanlow arranged that the first conference for supervisors would include key representatives from the supervisor and foreman groups. After the statement had been worked through in the usual way, the need to get started on implementation measures and thus to involve trade union officials and shop stewards was explained, and the problem of doing so before many supervisors themselves were involved was openly discussed. The result was agreement by the conference members that because of the circumstances no objection would be raised if early conferences were arranged for the trade union representatives. The method and timing of the events were also discussed and agreed.

In a similar way, the decision to shorten the formal conference period from two full days and an evening to one day and an evening for the later conferences in the series, gradually evolved from discussions with conference members about the best way to generate measures to put the philosophy into practice. The conclusion which emerged was that this could best be done in the work situation in people's own departments, rather than in mixed group discussions at a conference.

Shell Haven

From the start of their phase 2 dissemination programme, Shell Haven switched from the London hotel they had used for phase 1 to non-residential conferences in a local hotel, finding this the most convenient arrangement available in the area. They lasted two days, thus cutting out the preceding evening session, which Stanlow retained throughout, finding it a useful warm-up and introduction to the event.

During the second half of 1966, a series of twenty-one conferences was run for mixed groups of staff. From August onwards, after a briefing of the local trade union officials, and following a suggestion made at that meeting, three or four shop stewards were included in the membership of each conference. This was quite a different pattern from Stanlow's where special conferences had been arranged for shop stewards, and it reflected the refinery management's concern to ensure that all employees—including the shop stewards—could see they were getting the same treatment as everyone else.

In the first half of 1967, a further twenty conferences were run for junior staff and randomly selected hourly paid employees. The basis for this was a suggestion from the shop stewards: they did not want the conference experience limited only to shop stewards. They also asked that the process should cover all shop-floor employees. By the middle of 1967, about one-third of all hourly paid employees at Shell Haven had attended a two-day conference on the statement. After this, the remainder were covered by departmental discussions on site, led as at Stanlow by the department managers.

EFFECTS OF THE CONFERENCES

In general it seemed that the conferences achieved their objectives of imparting an understanding of the philosophy statement and of its implications for the way the company should run its affairs to achieve the best results. Clearly the level of understanding and commitment varied considerably among individuals. A minority, which included senior staff and shop stewards, were highly enthusiastic and anxious to get practical implementation measures started. These were the people who would help carry the programme forward. Another minority, some craft shop stewards at Shell Haven, rejected the document and refused to believe that the company seriously intended to put it into effect. It would have been surprising if this reaction had not appeared somewhere. Their reaction will be discussed more fully in Chapter 9.

The members of the Tavistock and ERP teams who had the opportunity of taking part in conferences at all the locations were able to gain a good overall impression of the dissemination process. They were struck with the way in which the document served to generate a wealth of different individual reactions and encouraged many people at all levels to speak their minds openly. They were impressed with the seriousness with which people discussed the issues raised by the statement and the importance they clearly attibuted to them. There was no suggestion that people thought they were playing games. They were impressed also with the great enthusiasm of some conference members, particularly at Stanlow, and their determination to push the programme forward. It seemed clear that the content of the statement was responding to a real need felt by many people in the organisation.

There were, of course, also a few negative aspects of the process.

For example, the enthusiasm and high level of expectation that changes would quickly come about contained the danger of disillusion, if things did not move forward as quickly as was hoped. Some people, although accepting the statement as valid, and accepting the commitment of the company's management to put it into effect, were doubtful whether there was genuine high level support for the programme in the Group. This fear was frequently raised at conferences and the management's explanations of what the managing director had done on this point did not appear always to dispose of all the doubts.

Some people also undoubtedly left the conferences with a distorted view of what the statement was all about. It was to emerge later that a minority of people in the supervisory ranks had interpreted it as a philosophy of "being nice to people," which they feared would have an adverse effect on discipline. The semi-jocular remark of a foreman overheard during a break at a refinery conference should doubtless be seen in this context. His comment to a colleague was: "I'll optimise the bastards!"

In spite of the negative aspects, however, the verdict on the general outcome of the conference dissemination process must be that it was very successful. Indications of people's involvement in the process were the large number of additions and improvements suggested to the text of the statement itself and the many ideas put forward on implementation possibilities. These were only the visible results of long discussions about what the company—or the refinery—was trying to do and how it could do it better.

There was naturally much discussion of how the company could make better use of its human resources. A point which was often fed in for debate was the idea that a status distinction between staff and hourly paid employees was no longer justified. As the elimination of the distinction was a possible outcome of future productivity bargaining, it was clearly valuable to get the view of conference members on the matter. The general reaction was that provided terms and conditions of employment could be satisfactorily rationalised, there was no reason why everyone should not be employed on a staff basis.

The need for more effective training at all levels was highlighted at many conferences. An early practical response to this need was the strengthening of training staff in the company, not by increasing numbers but by appointing more senior people to the roles.

A suggestion by the head of personnel at Stanlow led to the setting up of a seminar to improve the general social science knowledge of senior members of the department and a few interested line managers. The seminars were led by one of the Tavistock team and took place usually twice a month, during an extended lunch break. When Tavistock and ERP were developing a simplified method of socio-technical analysis at Stanlow in 1967, some seminar members took part and progress was regularly reported back to the full seminar, which acted as a valuable sounding-board.

Another practical response to the implications of the statement was the appointment at Shell Haven of a "resource manager," responsible for co-ordinating refinery efforts to match the recruitment, training and development of employees more effectively to planned changes in the technical system. He was also responsible for co-ordinating the production of objectives at refinery, department and unit levels, all of which had to be consistent with the company's stated economic and social objectives. This appointment was an important demonstration of the refinery general manager's commitment to implementation of the philosophy. One effect it had was to dispel the doubts, evident at the phase 1 conferences, about Shell Haven's future life.

An example of the resource manager's activities was the extension to operators due to become surplus as the result of the shut-down of old units, of wider opportunities than before to find alternative jobs: some older operators, for example, successfully took IBM tests and were transferred to the refinery computer centre.

A benefit from the conference process which had not been anticipated was the significant personal development which many senior staff demonstrated as a result of leading conference discussions on the draft statement. It was the management's view that such people had got more value from this experience than they would have done from attending any outside course in management over a comparable period. Another benefit was the tremendous gain in stature and influence which the general managers and their senior colleagues derived from their participation in the conference process and their visibility to and personal contact with all levels of employees.

Chapter 9

Involving the Trade Unions

Whilst everyone agreed that the support of the trade unions had to be secured if the development programme was to move forward, there were some misgivings about how they might react. The last occasion on which the company had faced them with something new had been two years previously when the intention to reduce the number of employees at the refineries had been announced. That event had caused considerable resentment among some trade union representatives and was not likely to have encouraged them to listen sympathetically to any further new ideas the company might wish to put in front of them. The meeting with the trade unions was therefore seen as another critical event which had to succeed if the programme was to continue.

APPROACH TO TRADE UNION OFFICIALS

The first approach was made at Stanlow, where the urgency was greatest. The refinery general manager had decided he would set up some pilot projects and the level of enthusiasm to get changes started was also highest there. Accordingly, the local officials from the craft unions listed in Appendix 1, the local and regional officials of the TGWU and the USDAW official representing laboratory staff, were all invited to attend a conference in May 1966 at Ruthin Castle, the same hotel Stanlow had used for its previous philosophy conferences. The programme was scheduled for an evening and a day, and it was gratifying to Stanlow management that almost all the officials invited, although extremely busy men, were able to attend. Once more, the opportunities which this event afforded for informal discussion on the first night were very valuable.

The objective of the conference was, of course, different from previous ones. It was not sought to get the commitment of the trade union officials to the statement of objectives and philosophy, but rather to explain to them what the company was trying to do, and what the general implications were for their members employed at the refinery. More specifically, it was hoped to get their agreement to the setting up of the pilot projects and of the joint working parties, each seen as a means of putting the philosophy into practice.

The initial procedure adopted was similar to that of previous conferences. The officials were given a copy of the draft statement and the general manager led a discussion on its contents and implications. Inevitably, there was some suspicion on the part of some of the officials about Stanlow's motives. It was asked, for example, whether the statement was a new way of securing more inter-craft flexibility, or was a precursor to another cut-back in numbers.

Another concern which was voiced was whether, if the company was able to achieve all it was setting out to do, including perhaps the wholesale transfer of hourly paid employees to staff status, the management had in mind a situation where trade union membership would become unnecessary in the future. In the course of the discussion it was possible to assure the officials that the company had no ulterior motives. There were no plans to reduce numbers further, except as a gradual evolutionary process where the work-load permitted it, nor did the management have any wish or intention of bringing about a change in the existing pattern of union representation on the refinery. If one outcome of productivity bargaining was to bring staff status to the hourly paid employees, the company would expect the same unions to continue to act as before on behalf of their members.

By the end of the discussions the early suspicions appeared to have been removed. The officials clearly had a good understanding of the company's real motives and intentions, and sympathised with what the management was setting out to do. Indeed there was a keen appreciation of the concepts used in the statement and the officials made it clear that they were favourably impressed with the whole approach and would lend it their support. Contributory factors to this positive outcome were undoubtedly the obvious sincerity of the Stanlow management and the presence of the Tavistock representatives with their professional objectivity. Most important was the progressive and receptive attitude of the majority of the trade union officials present.

The intention to set up some pilot projects was explained, and the hope that they would lead to redesign of jobs which would result in greater job satisfaction on the one hand and higher productivity on the other. The Tavistock representatives described the work they were involved in in Norway and the role the trade unions were playing there. This was to lead to a visit to Norway, later in 1966, of a small group from Stanlow, including managers, shop stewards and union officials, to meet some of the people involved there in the industrial democracy project and exchange experiences with them. In the meantime, the officials at the conference raised no objections to the proposed pilot projects at Stanlow.

They also accepted the idea that joint working parties should be set up, with freedom to discuss changes in the whole field of terms and conditions of work. They were, however, naturally anxious to have it established that the activities of the joint working parties would not in any way constitute negotiation with the company, which would have to be dealt with between the management and the union officials in the normal manner. They were also concerned that they should be kept fully informed about progress made by the working parties and they were given an undertaking that this would be done.

Some of the officials were personally sympathetic, in informal discussion, to the idea that the craft and the TGWU shop stewards should meet jointly in one working party, instead of in two separate parties. When this question was raised in the open meeting, however, it was not agreed by everyone present. The craft and TGWU stewards had split up several years previously and now traditionally conducted separate discussions with the management on any issue. It would, therefore, have been a major change in practice if agreement on a single joint working party had been reached. It was left that the matter would be raised again at the shop stewards' conference scheduled for the following month.

Another problem which was openly discussed was the question of job security at Stanlow. The 1964 reduction in numbers had given rise to feelings of insecurity among some employees and the management was considering putting out a policy statement on the subject to remove unnecessary fears. The basis of the policy statement was the company's commitment to protect and develop its human resources. This was seen as implying an obligation to ensure that any employee who became redundant, and who could not be retrained or redeployed within the organisation, should be returned to the labour market with at least as high a level of capability as when he joined the company. It was envisaged that this would entail helping any such redundant employee to find alternative employment, or possibly providing training to equip him to do so, where this seemed appropriate.

The reaction of one of the trade union officials present was to ask for a positive guarantee of no redundancy in the future. The majority, however, thought that this was unrealistic. They considered that the proposed policy statement represented a very fair attitude on the part of the company, provided there was prior consultation with union representatives on any occasion when the policy had to be put into effect.

The Stanlow conference was the first step taken to involve the trade unions in the company development programme. It appeared to be very successful. It demonstrated that the statement of objectives and philosophy made sense to trade union officials and, that after exploring its implications for them in their own roles, they were willing to support the company in its efforts. It initiated a new level of openness and frankness in the company's relationships with the officials and undoubtedly made possible a greater degree of mutual understanding. At the suggestion of the officials, it was agreed that a further meeting would be held after six months to review jointly how things were developing.

Other approaches to union officials

Shell Haven and Ardrossan also in due course invited their own local union officials to a discussion on-site about the philosophy statement. Both events went well, although at Shell Haven a number of the officials invited were unable to be present owing to the pressure of other business. In the shorter time available, there was less discussion of the statement and its implications than had been possible at Stanlow, but at neither location did the officials raise any objections to the setting up of joint working parties to provide a basis for productivity bargaining.

At head office level, meetings were arranged with the national officials of the TGWU and of the craft unions with which the refineries had agreements. As at the refinery meetings, the response to the company's intentions was sympathetic and supportive.

The fact that the union officials knew about the company's development programme, and supported its aims, undoubtedly contributed to some helpful actions on their part, later in the programme. For example, at Stanlow, when the productivity bargain with the craft unions had been signed, the officials circulated a message urging their members to do their best to make the deal really effective in practice. Further, when the company was encountering difficulties in reaching agreement with the TGWU that bargaining arrangements should be decentralised to the refineries, it was the national union officials' knowledge of the company development programme which helped to resolve the difficulties and to bring into being the local agreements the company was seeking.

INVOLVING THE SHOP STEWARDS

Following their successful conference with trade union officials, Stanlow held two conferences for their senior shop stewards. For these, the programme was scheduled to last an evening and two days. Present at the conferences were the refinery general manager and other management representatives, some overlap staff from previous conferences, including foremen and supervisors, and approximately twenty-four senior shop stewards representing the three major unionised groups of employees: craftsmen, operators and laboratory staff. Members of Tavistock and ERP were also present.

The first conference was another unique event in Stanlow's history. It was characterised by open speaking by all present and a high level of understanding and participation on the part of the shop stewards. The time was spent in the following way:

Day 1 evening	Full group	Introduction by general manager. Discussion of philosophy statement.
Day 2	2 sub-groups	Continued discussion of statement, general manager and deputy as chairman.
	Shop stewards (no others present)	Formulation of reactions to the statement.
	Full group	Reporting back by shop stewards of their views on statement.
Day 3	Full group	General manager in chair: working through implementation ideas (pilot projects and joint working parties) and draft policy statement on job security.

H

Shop stewards group	Formulation of reactions to implementation ideas and draft policy statement.
Full group	Reporting back by shop stewards. Conclusion by general manager.

In the course of working through the philosophy statement there was some initial suspicion among the shop stewards (as there had been among the officials) about the company's motives. Some wondered if this approach was a prelude to another run-down in manpower, others whether the company was embarking on this route as a result of the lack of success in completing the flexibility deal which had started in 1964. These suspicions were to be completely dispelled by the end of the conference.

During the first evening session, when such matters as developing people's potentialities and meeting their psychological needs were discussed, the shop stewards quoted many examples of cases where this had not been done in the past. They referred to instances of poor planning by managers, the stifling of initiative and the curtailment of decision making among craftsmen, the lack of information on the shop floor, and the inadequacy of training facilities. They also referred to what they thought were unsafe working practices.

Whilst to some extent, the shop stewards were "letting off steam" in voicing these complaints, it was recognised that many of the cases quoted represented clear examples of failure to apply the principle of joint optimisation. Moreover, they served to confirm the validity of one of the assumptions upon which the whole development programme had been based: namely, that in the past, inadequate use had been made of the capabilities of people at shop-floor level and that, as a result, many of them had adopted negative attitudes towards their jobs. They also demonstrated that the psychological needs listed in the philosophy statement were indeed relevant and important to the shop stewards and their colleagues.

When the whole statement had been worked through and the shop stewards reported their reactions to it, they said that they all understood the document and wished to support it. It was evident in fact that several of the shop stewards were very enthusiastic about its contents.

The final day's discussion of Stanlow's implementation intentions also produced positive results. Co-operation with the pilot projects was promised and with the joint working parties. Before the management had raised the possibility of merging the craftsmen and operators in one joint group, the shop stewards themselves volunteered this, suggesting that with a single working party representing the whole of the shop floor, it would be easier to develop change proposals applicable across the refinery. This appeared to be a significant step towards more collaborative attitudes. They made it clear, however, that the idea would have to be ratified by their own wider bodies and this, in the event, was never achieved.

Other matters discussed included Stanlow's proposed policy statement on job security, the desirability of eliminating overtime working and plans for improved training programmes for shop-floor employees. The question of how best to disseminate the philosophy statement to the mass of the shop-floor workers was explored, and led to the shop stewards expressing their concern about how they could explain to their colleagues back on the refinery what the conference had been all about. This was recognised as a real problem and it was agreed that a notice should be drafted for publication on the refinery, giving a brief account of the conference and its outcome.

A small *ad hoc* team forthwith produced a draft which was agreed by all present, including the shop stewards, as a reasonable summary of what had taken place. It was then circulated on the refinery as a special bulletin. Since it gives a flavour of the atmosphere and understanding which was achieved at the conference, its contents are reproduced below:

SPECIAL STANLOW BULLETIN –

COMPANY STATEMENT OF OBJECTIVES AND MANAGEMENT PHILOSOPHY

A conference between representatives of management and senior shop stewards took place at Manchester on 8–10 June 1966. The purpose of the conference was to work through the draft company statement of objectives and management philosophy which is being developed and to discuss ways in which it might be put into effect, taking into account the considerable expansion planned at Stanlow on both the oil and chemicals sides.

The result of the conference was that the senior shop stewards expressed their understanding of the company's philosophy and their support of it as a statement of intent.

It is not the intention to publish this statement since it is long and complex and needs considerable discussion to understand it fully. However, a copy of the statement is available with department managers and with the secretaries of the Foremen's Association and of the TGWU, Craft Union and USDAW stewards' committees.

The problem of how best to bring about an understanding of the philosophy to all employees is under joint consideration.

What we are trying to do is to make Stanlow a more satisfying, more efficient and more profitable place in which to work. We believe we can best do this by enabling everyone to participate more fully in planning and carrying out their work. This should lead not only to more job satisfaction but to improved efficiency. Any benefits resulting from this will be shared and of course where appropriate the way the sharing is to be done will be decided through normal collective bargaining machinery.

The implementation of these ideas will take time. However, one example of putting them into effect will be the setting up of a number of pilot studies to look at problem areas and through joint consultation with all levels of employees to make agreed changes to improve the organisation of work. In these pilot studies we shall be helped by the Tavistock Institute of Human Relations who have a great deal of experience in this field.

It is hoped also that another way of implementing will be the development of changes in terms and conditions of service taking into consideration any recommendations of the joint working parties.

A third example will be in the joint development of systematic and comprehensive training schemes for all levels of employees.

There will be many others and as they develop those concerned will be put in the picture.

The second conference for shop stewards followed a similar programme and achieved similarly favourable results.

Involving shop stewards at Shell Haven
The management at Shell Haven again decided to pursue a different strategy from Stanlow. Rather than arranging a conference specifically for shop stewards, they decided to invite a small number of shop stewards—usually three or four—to the regular series of conferences being held for mixed groups of staff. In view of the poor industrial relations situation, this new way of involving shop-floor

employees in the dissemination process seemed right for Shell Haven. In this way, the stewards would see that they were being treated in the same way as everyone else and could not suspect that they might be getting a specially doctored message. A disadvantage of this method of involving the shop stewards was that their presence occasionally seemed to have an inhibiting effect on some of the foreman and supervisors, who were reluctant to voice their own criticisms of the organisation, in competition as it were with the stewards. On the other hand, it was valuable for the management to be able to explore reactions to such notions as staff status for all employees, or the elimination of overtime working, with both supervisory and clerical staff and shop-floor people present.

The reactions of the shop stewards at Shell Haven to the philosophy statement were very mixed. The majority were in favour of it and willing to support the company's efforts to put it into practice. The senior shop stewards of the TGWU in particular were very enthusiastic. They saw as a major implication of the statement the possibility of developing a much more participative style of resolving problems on the refinery and welcomed the idea of the joint working party as a mechanism for collaborative efforts, where the shop stewards could make a significant contribution to the outcome. The feeling with which they left the philosophy conference seemed, therefore, to be that the company had finally produced in its draft statement ideas about making more effective use of people which they themselves had for a long time known to be necessary. They were to carry this initial enthusiasm through to their participation in the operators' joint working party, and in the development of a productivity bargain.

By contrast, the leading craft shop stewards refused to accept that the company seriously intended to put its new philosophy into practice. They seemed to interpret the whole project as a subtle attempt to "brainwash" people into accepting further reductions in manpower and other undesirable changes. Although this view was not shared by all the craft shop stewards and although most, if not all, the individual craftsmen who attended subsequent conferences appeared to support the statement and the company's intentions, it was the suspicious attitude of the leading shop stewards which was to carry through into the craft joint working party. In a sense, this craft working party at Shell Haven represented an unplanned "control" alongside the other joint working parties, since it was the only one whose shop steward members had rejected the philosophy statement and were to insist on using the working party as a mechanism for bargaining. As described in Chapter 14, it was also the only one which produced completely negative results.

CONCLUSION

With the exception of the small but influential group of senior craft shop stewards at Shell Haven, and perhaps one or two individual officials at Stanlow, the general reaction of trade union representatives to the company's development programme was highly encouraging. In general, the two major implications which emerged for them were welcomed: namely, the company's intention to develop people's potentialities and build more satisfying jobs; and the intention to rationalise terms and conditions of employment so that, among other things, their members would enjoy a more stable level of income.

The willingness of the management to discuss its plans and future intentions and how these would affect unionised employees was also appreciated by the trade union officials and helped to create a more open climate, even where this had been good before.

When, in 1967, the craftsmen at Stanlow went on strike over an issue not directly related to the development programme—the issue of unionisation of craft foremen and supervisors—the managers who negotiated a return to work with the union officials reported a marked increase in the ability on both sides to confront the problem openly and squarely. They considered this had led to a more satisfactory and lasting solution to the problem than might otherwise have been possible.

Part Four
PUTTING THEORY INTO PRACTICE

Chapter 10

General Strategy of Implementation

The process of disseminating the company philosophy down the line, described in Part 3, had been largely successful in securing acceptance by most employees involved of the ideas and concepts embodied in the draft statement. The next, and more difficult, stage was to get the ideas translated into action and put into practice in the work situation.

The two stages were not, of course, separate and sequential: implementation measures had to overlap the continuing process of dissemination. Furthermore, just as there had been no blue-print laying down the way the dissemination conferences were to be organised, so there was no neat predetermined package of implementation measures to be put into effect. Rather, it was foreseen, the small group of enthusiasts at each location would, under the leadership of the location manager, and with the assistance of Tavistock and ERP, develop an action programme along the lines which seemed most appropriate to them.

It was envisaged that the various locations would tend, because of their widely differing circumstances, to develop quite different methods of implementation. Such diversity, it was thought, would be useful, since a broader field of possible implementation measures could be explored than if all were following the same path. Provided each location could learn from what was happening at the others, the overall benefit to the company would be greater.

GUIDELINES FOR IMPLEMENTATION

Although there were no rules for implementation, the statement itself did offer managers a number of guidelines. It made it clear that one of management's key tasks was to create conditions in which employees at all levels could become committed to their tasks and could accept responsibility for achieving their objectives.

This indicated two clear focal points for action. First, creating satisfactory working conditions, in which productivity bargaining would play an important role; and, secondly, applying the principle of joint optimisation to redesign jobs where this was necessary to enable people to meet their psychological needs more effectively.

There were a number of other areas where action was also seen to be needed. For example, there was a need to establish operational and social objectives down the line, consistent with the agreed company objectives; to establish mechanisms for ensuring that people knew what their own objectives were and how well they were achieving them; and for adequate communication links to enable people to do their jobs properly.

However, in the end it would be a question of people, as section 7 of the statement put it, "searching out the implications for themselves." This was indeed the way the implementation programme was to develop, with a range of activities, all fitting into the overall framework provided by the philosophy statement.

MAIN CHANNELS OF IMPLEMENTATION

By mid-1966, four main channels in which implementation measures were expected to develop had been identified. They are described briefly below and in more detail in the next four chapters.

1 Pilot projects (Chapter 11). These were to be carefully planned experiments on the lines of the Norwegian field experiments described in Chapter 3. As the settings were different from those of previous experiments, different problems could be expected to arise. The pilot projects as they developed would demonstrate how the principle of joint optimisation could be put into practice in an existing refinery. It was intended that the projects would serve as models on the basis of which other managers at Stanlow and at the other refineries would be able to try out innovations in their own departments, thus in due course increasing the level of joint optimisation achieved throughout the organisation.

2 Department managers as change agents (Chapter 12). In parallel with the planned changes spreading from the pilot projects, it was anticipated that a number of managers would wish to initiate changes within their units which they had thought of by themselves, for example, by examining how far existing jobs were meeting psychological needs and making changes so that they could be more effectively met. It was hoped that this would lead to a wave of self-generated improvements across the company. Department managers were seen as the most important people in this implementation channel, since they typically controlled an identifiable socio-technical system and were responsible for the plant and the people who made up that system. It was hoped that the departmental meetings held to discuss the philosophy statement with hourly paid employees would also serve to generate implementation measures.

3 Designing a new refinery (Chapter 13). The fact that the company was planning a new refinery on Teesside at the time the development programme started up was seen as a great opportunity to try out its principles in practice on a green field site. It was possible to design the social system whilst the final design for the highly computerised and automated technical system was still emerging and thus to try out the principle of joint optimisation on the grand scale. It also offered the opportunity to build up from scratch an appropriate set of terms and conditions of employment. It was hoped that the new refinery would become an ideal organisation towards which the existing refineries could aim.

4 Joint working parties (Chapter 14). An important outcome of the company development programme was always seen to be the successful negotiation of productivity bargains which would reflect the beneficial effects of the dissemination of the philosophy statement. The setting-up of the joint working parties in the refineries was, therefore, recognised as an implementation measure the success or failure of which might critically affect the quality of the bargains to be struck with the trade unions.

UTILISATION OF SPECIAL RESOURCES

Each location had nominated a person to co-ordinate all its activities connected with the development programme: at Ardrossan, it was the personnel manager, at Shell Haven, the resource manager, and at Stanlow, an engineer from the line. The role of the Tavistock and ERP teams in the implementation phase was to collaborate with these people and to lend location managements advice or practical assistance wherever this was requested. In addition, they had the task of mapping what was happening by way of implementation across the company and keeping each location informed about the experiences gained by others. They were also asked by the managing director to carry out an assessment of progress on his behalf early in 1967, the results of which are described in Chapter 16.

As the implementation programme progressed, Tavistock and ERP tended to devote most of their efforts to assisting developments at Stanlow. This was because the pilot projects were located there and led to further socio-technical experiments, whereas Shell Haven concentrated more on achieving satisfactory bargains with the trade unions, for which they did not need outside assistance. Their industrial relations problem was far more serious than at Stanlow and dealing with it was their first priority.

Chapter 11

Pilot Projects

One of the focal points for putting the philosophy into practice was the redesign of jobs. The objective was to provide people with jobs from which, whilst effectively meeting the technical requirements, they could also derive sufficient psychological satisfaction to become committed to doing their task well.

What was needed, therefore, was a method of analysing existing jobs which would show to what extent they needed redesigning and would indicate the sort of changes which could be made. Tavistock's suggestion was that the method of socio-technical analysis being applied at several Norwegian sites at that time would be an appropriate tool to use for this purpose. Although it was a rather complex and lengthy process, it had proved an effective method of improving the design of jobs and of allowing people at all levels in an organisation to learn what this involved.

The general manager at Stanlow accordingly decided to try out the method on an experimental basis. Planning meetings were held at Stanlow during May 1966 to decide which of a number of suggested sites for a project would be most appropriate and how the projects should be set up and manned. It was recognised that a lot of help and guidance would be needed from the Tavistock team, but it was hoped to build much of the necessary expertise into the company by involving Stanlow personnel people and ERP in the projects from the start. It was decided to run three projects, all with different characteristics, and a start was made on them in July 1966, after agreement had been reached with the trade union officials and shop stewards.

CHOICE OF SITES

Of the three sites chosen for projects, two were to provide opportunities for socio-technical analysis of differing complexity whilst the third was aimed at discovering ways of improving performance in the area of engineering maintenance, through a study of the interface problems between engineering and process operations. The chosen sites were as follows:

1 Distillation unit. This was selected as an example of the key processing units on the refinery, sited at the heart of its technology. Its technical system was very complex. The socio-technical analysis would require a high level of participation by the Tavistock team. If the project showed that performance on the unit could be improved by enhancing the degree of joint optimisation, it was envisaged that similar improvements could be spread to other process units in the company.

2 Lub-oil installation. This was a department responsible for blending and packaging lubricating oils, where the technical system was relatively simple. It provided an example of the more labour intensive technologies which were likely to persist for the foreseeable future, in some of the ancillary operations on the refinery. It was chosen in part because the department manager wanted to take some action and considered there was room for improved performance from the people in the system. Because of the simple technology, it was envisaged that much of the work on the analysis could be carried out by the people in the department, with general guidance from Tavistock on the method of tackling it. It was seen, therefore, as a "self-help" project, which would serve as an example to other department managers who wanted to bring about changes in their own departments with limited expert help from outside.

3 Engineering maintenance. Unlike the other two projects, this one would not be focused on a particular unit, but would be a study of the relationship between the engineering and the operating functions. This relationship had received much attention in the past but it was felt it required re-examination because of the scope for improvement and because plant reliability was becoming increasingly important. The hope was that a small team of senior engineers and operating managers working with Tavistock representatives would, through a reappraisal of the role of the engineering department and a redefinition of its objectives, be able to recommend organisational changes which would lead to a more effective allocation of maintenance resources.

Preparatory steps

After deciding on the specific projects, a number of preparatory steps had to be taken before they could be launched. For example, Tavistock had to ensure that there would be sufficient expert help available to man them, particularly the complex distillation unit project. In addition to their own participation, under the overall direction of Hans van Beinum, they therefore arranged for a Norwegian social scientist, Per Engelstad, who had worked on the socio-technical projects in Norway and Leo Smythe, an Irish social scientist who had worked with van Beinum on the Dublin transport project, to come to Stanlow for six months to assist with the distillation unit study. To help with the lub-oil installation project the services of a Dutch social scientist from Utrecht, Jan Schaaij, who had worked with van Beinum on a socio-technical study in the Dutch Telecommunications industry, were secured for a similar period. And, finally, Lou Davis, a visiting professor from UCLA joined the team on the engineering study on a part-time basis. He was an engineer of wide experience before becoming an organisational scientist, who had adopted a socio-technical approach.

Care had also to be taken to make sure that everyone who would be involved in, or affected by, the projects knew what they were all about. This applied particularly to the distillation unit and the lub-oil installation, where all levels of employee would be concerned, including the shop floor. The purpose of the projects was described in the context of putting the philosophy into practice.

At the same time, it was made clear that the projects were experimental. There was still much to learn about carrying out this type of analysis and problems would undoubtedly develop. It was envisaged that after the initial analysis of the existing system, changed methods of operation would be agreed for a trial period. If they were successful, they would continue, but if not the system would revert as far as possible to its previous method of operation.

In the distillation unit and lub-oil installation projects a steering committee was established with the department manager at its head, and representatives from various levels of the department and the shop floor. The outside experts worked through these committees.

Two safeguards were given to all employees whose jobs might be changed: first, it was established that no one would become redundant as the result of any changes introduced (although it might be necessary to move to a different job); and, second, no employee would receive less money during the trial period than his average earnings over a reasonable period prior to the project.

RESULTS OF THE PROJECTS

An important feature of the projects was that they were taking place in real life situations on the refinery and were exposed to all the day-to-day operating problems and pressures. All of them encountered unforeseen delays and the engineering study was to be suspended before reaching the action stage. Work on the distillation unit analysis, for example, was held up by a fire which, incidentally, occurred before any changes in operating methods had been introduced. Nevertheless, the projects produced valuable results. These are described below, in some detail for the distillation unit project and more briefly for the other two.

Distillation unit
The work was planned in two phases. Phase 1 would involve the analysis of the unit as a socio-technical system and recommendations for improved methods of operation. Phase 2 would include a trial period of running the unit under experimental new conditions.

Phase 1 took about six months to complete. Tavistock produced a report in February 1967 giving the results of the analysis and recommendations for the sort of changes to be built into an action programme.

Essentially, the main conclusion of the report was that the process operators and shift chargehands had the capability to control the unit more effectively than at present and thus to bring about a higher level of performance. In order to achieve this, it was suggested, the process operators needed additional training, a better understanding of operational objectives, more information about operating targets, more freedom to take decisions and better team work. It was argued that if these changes were introduced, the effect would be not only a higher level of performance on the unit but also more satisfying jobs for the operators and more commitment on their part to meet operational targets. A further effect would be a need to make changes in the existing roles of the shift foreman, the supervisor, and the departmental technologist.

Contents of distillation unit report. Looked at in a little more detail, the report included the following sections:

1   A study of the technical system, identifying its special characteristics

and the types of demand it imposed on the people responsible for operating and controlling it.

2 A study of the social system, the people who ran the unit, and the way they were organised. This section included the results of two group interviews conducted with the process operators. Their views about such matters as their own jobs, the management structure of the department and the system of engineering maintenance on the unit were reported on an anonymous basis.

3 An outline of the interdependencies between the technical and the social systems, together with their implications for ways in which the level of joint optimisation could be improved. For example:

(a) Both the flammable nature of the materials processed on the unit and the stress likely to be caused when operating the unit in "unsteady" conditions implied the need to build a stable team of operators with confidence in each other's skills and capabilities.

(b) The dispersal of the operators in separate places on the unit (for example, in the panel room, the pumphouse and the heaters), reinforced the need for a stable shift-team and implied the need for the operators to work towards the same overall unit objectives, rather than specific objectives relating only to their own tasks.

(c) The fact that the continuous twenty-four hours a day operations had to be covered by three separate shifts of operators implied a need for a collaboration between the shifts, rather than competitiveness, and twenty-four hour performance targets shared by all three shifts, rather than targets relating to the eight-hour shifts.

(d) The high level of mechanisation and instrumentation on the unit meant that the main contribution from the operators was effecting control: this implied the need for the operators to have an intimate knowledge of the unit, wide operating experience and the ability to take information, exercise judgement and make speedy and accurate decisions.

4 Recommendations on the way in which changes might be introduced. It was suggested that changes were required at three levels:

(a) At the level of the individual, the need was to improve the operators' knowledge and understanding of the process and to provide them with a broader picture of refinery operations as they affected the distillation unit.

(b) At the level of the shift crew, the need was to help develop effective team performance. This would entail reducing the amount of movement of operators between units so that stable shift teams could be

I

built. It would also involve increasing the capability for interchanging tasks on the unit between the team members. There was a need to establish team targets in relation to the twenty-four hour period, not to their own eight-hour shift. There was a need, finally, to encourage the shift team, through training and better communications, to acquire a similar picture of the unit's function and objectives to that held by the department manager. The study had shown that whereas the department manager was seeking to optimise unit performance, and saw continual adjustment of the unit to meet changing conditions and demands as a means to that end, the operators saw the attainment of maximum throughput as an objective and sought therefore to maintain steady state conditions, avoiding adjustment, for as long as possible.

(c) At the level of the department it was suggested that the existing organisation would need to be modified if the shift teams were to develop improved capability for dealing with most of the variances arising on the unit. The existing role of the shift foreman would, for example, become unnecessary. It was also recommended that new communication links between the management of the department and the operators should be developed, so that the shift teams could become more involved in working towards shared objectives and targets and more committed to achieving a higher level of unit performance.

Outcome of the project. The general reaction to the report was that the analysis was valid and that the recommendations were worth trying out in practice. For various reasons, however, there was a long delay before a final action programme was developed. The task of developing it was the responsibility of the department manager with advice and assistance from his steering committee. An unavoidable change in departmental managers meant that in spite of the enthusiasm of the new manager, an action programme was not finalised until mid-1967. The new department manager considered the report's recommendations held out good possibilities of improving the level of performance of the unit. Within a short time after his appointment, he produced a comprehensive action plan built on the project's findings.

In the meantime, the delay had led to considerable frustration on the part of the operators, who had developed high expectations about possible changes on the unit. Furthermore, as the result of the activities of the joint working parties, refinery-wide discussions had begun to take place on issues which it was thought might be built into a productivity deal covering all operators. When the proposed action plan was eventually discussed with the distillation unit operators they took the view that some of its proposals overlapped with those which were likely to be the subject of productivity bargaining. They thought it was preferable therefore to await the outcome of the bargaining, rather than to adopt new methods in isolation on the distillation unit. The proposals relating to building stable shift teams and increasing inter-role capabilities on the unit had, therefore, to be dropped from the action plan.

In spite of this set-back, however, a number of changes were put into effect by the department manager. It was his later view, and that of the refinery management, that these changes had made a favourable impact on performance within the department. They included:

1   The development of objectives for the department, the unit, the shift teams and the individual operators. These were discussed and agreed with the shift teams
2   Improved training for the individual operators, including information about the supply and market situations, operating targets and technical developments
3   Tutoring for the shift teams by the technical staff in the department, using case studies to improve their knowledge of operations and their capability for problem solving
4   Changes in the roles of the departmental technologist and the shift foreman
5   Improvements in the system of communications between the managerial and the operating levels in the department

Lub-oil installation
The general approach to this project was similar to that followed in the distillation unit project but the system to be studied, and consequently the data involved, were far less complicated. A further advantage was that the employees concerned were all day-workers so that the problem of communicating with night-shift workers did not arise.

The phase 1 analysis of the technical system was carried out largely by the deputy department manager, with guidance from the Tavistock representative, and the assistance of the supervisors and charge-hands in each section. They produced a map of the technology and the work flow and a list of the main variances which had to be controlled by the people in the department.

Analysis of the existing social system was handled mainly by the Tavistock representative. As on the distillation unit, group interviews were held with the operatives and resulted in this case in a large number of suggestions for improvements in the way various jobs were carried out. A survey of the views of the supervisors in the department was also conducted. The next stage was to consider, with the steering committee, in what ways the employees available could be better organised and utilised to meet the demands of the technical system in the most efficient way. As in the distillation unit project, however, there was once more considerable delay in producing an action plan. This caused frustration among the operatives involved, some of whom had shown great enthusiasm over the project.

An action plan was eventually developed outlining a number of changes to be introduced in the small packaging section of the department. A feature of the plan was the valuable contribution of the operatives, since many of their suggestions had been incorporated in it. The proposals were all relatively small and simple. They fell into two classes. First were the proposals for minor improvements in the technical system, which by giving the operators better access to the equipment, and by modifying some items of equipment, made it easier for them to carry out their jobs. Second, there were a number of minor maintenance items which had previously been carried out by the engineering department but which were now to be included in the operator's tasks.

The introduction of these changes in the last quarter of 1967 led to a significant improvement in the section's productivity (of the order of 20 per cent). Furthermore, it was clear that the project had resulted in a great improvement in the quality of communication within the department and in a clearer perception by employees at all levels of the objectives they had to pursue.

Engineering maintenance
As already reported, this study was discontinued as a formal project at the end of 1966. This was not because of lack of progress—in fact some interesting and promising ideas had emerged—but rather because of the high pressure of other work on the refinery members of the team at that time and the lack of recorded data in the form needed for an empirical examination of the problem. Arrangements were made to produce the necessary data by logging over a period of time the different categories of maintenance carried out in one operating department and it was left that the project might be reopened at a later date. In fact, this did not occur. To re-examine the basic tasks and organisation of maintenance was perhaps too ambitious an undertaking for people

heavily loaded with day-to-day work. But it was their dissatisfaction with the existing system, and with the short-comings of engineering design, that had prompted them initially to propose the project.

CONCLUSIONS

The outcomes of the three pilot projects were therefore very different. The engineering study produced promising ideas but nothing of practical value. The potential benefits of the distillation unit project were only partially realised, although it led to a number of useful changes and produced lasting improvements in the level of effective communication in the department and in the extent of the process operators' involvement in the operation of the unit. These improvements, moreover, were to be adopted by other operating departments at Stanlow, thus meeting one of the original aims of the project. The lub-oil installation project, finally, had resulted in changes which successfully improved performance, albeit in a more modest field.

Certainly the experience gained through the pilot projects had demonstrated that socio-technical analysis was potentially a valuable tool for improving the motivation and performance of employees in a refinery environment. On the other hand, it had also demonstrated the difficulties of carrying out a complex and time-consuming process of analysis and of introducing changes in a situation of continual operational pressures and problems.

It was therefore decided to switch attention to the development of a simplified method of carrying out socio-technical analysis, which would take less time to apply, and would need less expert assistance from outside the department concerned. A further advantage of a simplified method and a shorter time-span would be that the people involved would be less likely to develop exaggerated expectations about the outcome. A lesson learned from the distillation unit project, in particular, was the need to guide people's expectations along reasonable paths. Changes which can enhance performance and job satisfaction do not have to be dramatic.

The way in which Tavistock and ERP developed a simplified method of socio-technical analysis in collaboration with Stanlow, is described in the next chapter. Also described is the work done on producing an alternative method—which was called role analysis—for use in a situation where there was no well-defined technical system as, for example, in a purely administrative department.

Chapter 12

Department Managers as Change Agents

Department managers were seen as the key people to put the ideas of the philosophy statement into practice. It was typically at this level of management that individuals were responsible for a well-defined socio-technical system. It was hoped that those of them who were most enthusiastic about the philosophy would start the process of implementation and that others would follow, and that in this way a wide front of implementation measures would develop across the company.

A number of department managers did indeed take early steps in their own departments. For example, at Stanlow the head of personnel had several sessions with his industrial relations manager and assistants, reviewing with them how far they felt their jobs were meeting their psychological needs. The result of these discussions was that changes were agreed in the job boundaries of the assistants and in the area in which they could take decisions. The new arrangements gave more effective coverage of the work and more satisfaction in their jobs to the men.

At Shell Haven the manager of the materials department decided fairly early in the dissemination programme to begin regular weekly discussions with his supervisors about the implications of the philosophy statement within the department. These discussions were later extended down the line to include the hourly paid employees. They had a positive and favourable effect in establishing a climate of more open communication, achieving a common understanding of departmental objectives and improving the solving of work problems as they arose. They also formed a pattern which other departments would in due course follow.

At Stanlow again, a good example of how the better utilisation of operators' capabilities could improve performance was provided by the micro-wax department. The manager began by holding weekly meetings with his supervisors and in due course extended them to include all the process operators. Over a period of time as a result of these discussions, the operators were given greater discretion to make decisions on the unit (for example, to adjust unit operating conditions to meet the daily programme) and the authority of the supervisor and foremen was also widened (for example, to include control of budget expenditure in their own spheres). Aided by some technical changes, the performance of the department and the morale of the employees improved significantly.

It became clear, however, that without some additional assistance and encouragement only a minority of department managers were likely to embark on change programmes on their own account. Apart from being key people in the change process, they were also very busy people, working often under considerable daily pressures. Some of them also volunteered that whilst the concept of joint optimisation made theoretical sense to them, they were uncertain how it could be put into practice in their own particular circumstances.

Three lines of action were therefore developed to assist the department managers:

1   Briefing sessions to consider how departmental meetings could best be run
2   Development of a simplified method of analysing a socio-technical system
3   Development of a method of role analysis

These three activities are described in the following sections of this chapter.

BRIEFING SESSIONS FOR DEPARTMENT MANAGERS

It had been decided, first at Stanlow and later at Shell Haven, to carry on the dissemination of the philosophy statement to junior staff and hourly paid employees through departmental meetings. It was anticipated that these discussions would establish platforms on which implementation programmes could be built.

In order to help department managers decide how these events could best be handled, a series of four briefing sessions was held at Stanlow in

September 1966 with Tavistock and ERP assisting. The idea was not to impose conformity but to explore possibilities. Each department manager was left free to run his own meetings as he thought fit.

Examples of the points which emerged from the briefing sessions were:

On dissemination

1   Many managers planned to incorporate discussion of the philosophy statement into their normal schedule of meetings, thus minimising the need for extra time
2   Some planned special meetings outside normal working hours
3   Some planned a phased process, involving first their supervisors, then the shop stewards, and then other hourly paid employees
4   Some planned to carry out the process jointly with other departments, with whom they had close working links
5   Most intended to use the simplified statement and some asked for material to help them explain to their employees the concept of joint optimisation

On implementation

6   There was general agreement on the need to get started quickly on some implementation items, even relatively small ones
7   No change should be made without ensuring that other departments would not be adversely affected
8   An approach put forward by Tavistock and ERP to reviewing a department's activities in a way which would indicate where changes were needed, was generally accepted as useful. It envisaged:
   (a) The establishment, and agreement at all levels, of department and sections' objective, which should be consistent with company and refinery objectives
   (b) A review of the activities of each section in the light of the agreed objectives
   (c) A review of individual roles in the light of the psychological needs listed in the philosophy statement

The outcome of these meetings was passed on to the other locations.

A SIMPLIFIED METHOD OF SOCIO-TECHNICAL ANALYSIS

The need for a simplified method of analysing an existing production system had become apparent during the formal pilot projects at Stanlow. The ERP representative who had participated in all the project teams was particularly keen to get a method which could be put down on paper and which could be taught to department managers.

In May 1967 he attended a conference at Lincoln, organised jointly by Tavistock and the Work Research Institute in Oslo, for social scientists from many countries who were interested in the socio-technical approach to organisation development. From this event he brought back the framework of a simplified method of socio-technical analysis which had been put forward by Fred Emery.

This framework was developed and tested out in collaboration with Stanlow, with the help of the members of the social science seminar. A small informal team was set up, including Michael Foster of Tavistock, some personnel people from Stanlow and the ERP members. It was found easier and more satisfactory to develop the method by applying it to an actual system, than to attempt to do it purely theoretically. An operating department manager offered the use of one of his small units for this purpose and briefed the team on its characteristics. Although not all the nine steps involved were tried out on the ground, the exercise indicated to the team and to the operating department manager that the method should work in practice.

In August 1967 the opportunity arose to test the method out further at the Work Research Institute in Oslo. Three members of the team went across there and worked through the steps in detail with the Institute director, Einar Thorsrud, and with Per Engelstad, who had assisted with the distillation unit project at Stanlow, as well as having had a lot of experience on the Norwegian projects. This proved a valuable exercise and the method was modified and further improved as a result of the visit.

Contents of the analytical method
A paper produced by ERP in October 1967 after the Oslo visit, which describes the nine step method in some detail, is reproduced in Appendix 5. Below is a summary of its contents and some notes of advice on how the method was to be applied in practice. Although it may still appear complicated, it became less so when related to an actual unit. The nine steps are:

1   Initial scanning. Obtaining a brief over-view of the production system and its environment. This should cover the geographical layout, the organisational structure, the main inputs and outputs, constraints on production, and the system's objectives.

2 *Identification of unit operations.* Each unit operation is largely self-contained and effects an identifiable transformation in the raw material, either in its properties or its location.

3 *Identification of key process variances and their interrelationships.* A key process variance is a major deviation from the normal or specified; it is likely to affect significantly the ability of the production system to meet its quality, quantity or cost targets.

4 *Analysis of the social system.* Examining the extent to which the social system is capable of controlling the main process variances and the extent to which the jobs meet psychological needs.

5 *Men's perceptions of their roles.* Obtaining the men's own perceptions of how their jobs meet psychological needs.

6 *Maintenance system.* Identifying the extent to which the maintenance system affects the capability of the production system to achieve its objectives; and considering to what extent maintenance tasks could be built into operating roles.

7 *Supply and user systems.* Identifying variances which are passed into the production system but arise in the supply or user systems, which may be adjacent departments in some cases, or in the outside world in others.

8 *Company environment and development plans.* Examining constraints on change which might be imposed by the wider company environment (e.g. company personnel policies) and considering implications of any plans for future development.

9 *Proposals for change.* Gathering together ideas for change which have emerged during the study and considering their viability for inclusion in an action programme.

People wishing to apply this method of analysis were advised to:

1   Select if possible a small unit rather than a large complex one
2   Concentrate on the existing production system, not on how it was
3   Avoid going into too much detail and identify only key information under each step
4   Set up a small action group headed by the manager of the unit involved, with representatives from all levels including the shop floor: the group would carry the analysis through and any outside help should be attached to it

5   Consider assigning one or more members of the action group to
     work full-time on the project for a period, since a great deal of
     effort and commitment would be needed to carry through the
     analysis and the ensuing action programme

Use of the method as a training tool
One reason for developing this method had been the desire to produce
something which could be taught to department managers in a training
situation, before they attempted to try it out in practice within their
own departments.

   An opportunity to test its usefulness as a training tool arose when
ERP was offered three days on the programme of several residential
courses run by the head office training department for department
managers from all locations. The three days were used by Tavistock
and ERP to:

1   Reinforce understanding of the key concepts of the philosophy
     statement
2   Discuss implementation measures already taken and future
     possibilities
3   Explain how the analytical nine-step method and the role analysis
     method (described later in this chapter) had been developed
4   Try out each method in two syndicates, taking as a basis for the
     exercise an operating unit or an administrative section managed
     by one of the syndicate members
5   Get reactions from the managers on the usefulness of the two
     methods

The general reaction to both the methods was very favourable. Some
managers from Shell Haven were particularly impressed, since they
knew less about the pilot project activities than their Stanlow colleagues.
It was the general view, however, that a department manager would
still need outside help (for example, from Tavistock or ERP) if he
wanted to apply either method successfully within his own department.
   In the meantime, the management at Stanlow (where a new refinery
manager had recently taken over) had asked for a demonstration of
the two methods. A two-day programme was arranged for them at the
end of October, so that the twenty senior managers could try out both
methods in syndicates.

The general reaction was again favourable but there was a concern that if the methods were taught to all the department managers at Stanlow, there would be insufficient expert help available to cope with the degree of interest and expectation which would probably be aroused. It was also considered that there was a need to establish that the use of the methods could in fact produce changes which would improve performance levels, before they were demonstrated on a wider scale to department managers.

It was agreed therefore that as the next move, both methods would be tried out in a practical situation at the refinery.

APPLYING THE NINE-STEP METHOD

In order to achieve quicker results, it was decided to do some more work on the study of the bitumen block moulding unit which had served originally to develop and test out the method, rather than to embark on a completely new project. Another reason for this decision was that there was indeed by late 1967 a drastic shortage of people available to help carry through a new project, owing to staff transfers affecting ERP, and the pressure of other work on the Stanlow personnel department.

The study was completed by the end of 1967. It was still not a comprehensive application of the method, since not all the steps had been fully carried out on the ground. Also, the knowledge that the unit was likely to be replaced by a more modern one within two years made people reluctant to contemplate expenditure on changes, especially in the technical system.

Nevertheless, in spite of these constraints, the study generated a number of proposals for change which give an idea of the sort of results which might emerge from the application of this analytical method. Before summarising the proposals it is necessary to give a brief and simplified description of the unit and its characteristics, so that the implications of the proposals can be understood. The diagram in Figure 12:1 will help to clarify this background information.

Description of bitumen block moulding unit
The bitumen block moulding operation is a relatively simple one. Essentially it involves spraying moulds with a release agent, then filling them with molten bitumen. The moulds are removed to cool overnight, then returned and broken open to release the solidified bitumen blocks.

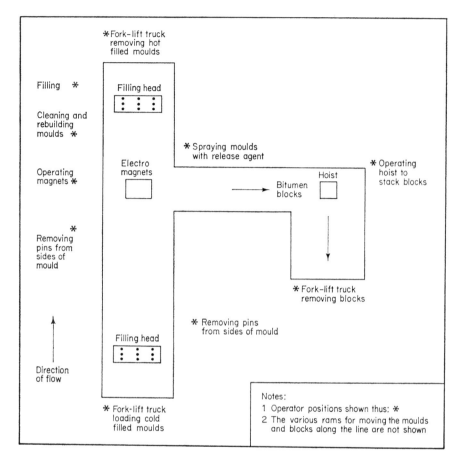

FIGURE 12:1 SCHEMATIC LAYOUT OF BITUMEN BLOCK MOULDING
UNIT AND OPERATOR POSITIONS

The unit consists of a production line with a filling head at each end
and in the centre an electro-magnetic lifting device. Opposite the electro-
magnets is an L-shaped branch for the off-loading of blocks. The line
can be operated from both ends. The unit is manned by ten operators,
of whom three drive fork-lift trucks. Their positions are shown on the
diagram. In addition, a chargehand has a part-time responsibility for the
unit.

The cycle of operations is as follows: the hot bitumen feedstock is
gravity fed to a filler head from one of five storage tanks located above
the production line. The filler operates a switch to fill a pre-sprayed

mould which has a separator grid dividing it into nine compartments. The filled mould is removed from the line by fork-lift truck and stored overnight to cool.

The following morning the cooled moulds are returned to the line. They are moved along the line by rams, pins are removed from their sides and with the aid of hammers and the electro-magnets the sides are collapsed and the separator grid is lifted out, leaving the nine bitumen blocks free to be off-loaded via the L-shaped branch.

The emptied mould and separator grid are scraped clean, reassembled and sprayed with release agent. The prepared mould is then pushed under the filler head again and the cycle is complete.

Results of analysis
Analysis of the key variances (those which could significantly affect the quality, quantity or cost of the product) arising from the technical system showed that among the most important ones were:

1   The temperature of the bitumen feed
2   The level of fill in the moulds
3   The position of the separator grids

If the bitumen was too hot when fed into the moulds, it caused the release agent to boil and lose its effectiveness. The result was that the following day it would be very difficult, or impossible, to remove the separator grid from the mould and the still full mould would have to be carted off somewhere for special attention at a later date. Overfilling the mould could have a similar effect, whilst underfilling it was a waste of productive capacity. Wrongly positioned separator grids in the moulds could also cause the bitumen to stick, or result in wrongly-shaped blocks.

Analysis of the social system showed that some of these key variances were only partly controlled by the existing system. The result was that about one in five of the moulds gave up its blocks only after great efforts with the hammers, or not at all. This entailed a considerable loss in production.

The analysis also showed that in the view of the department manager and the supervisor, psychological needs were not all adequately met in any of the jobs, and in some of them they were not met at all.

Proposals for change
The changes proposed related mainly to the social system. They were

aimed at a better control of the key variances with possibly enlarged and more satisfying roles for the operators. Not all the proposals are listed below but the principal ones are:

1 Elimination of chargehand role, and the enlargement of filler's role. This would involve transferring from the chargehand to the filler the responsibility for deciding which storage tanks to fill from and the authority to stop filling if he judged the feed to be too hot. Thus such devices as existed to control the bitumen temperature variance would be placed in the hands of the filler.

The chargehand's other main task on the unit—switching the operation of the rams when the direction of the production line was changed each day—would have to be carried out by the operators.

2 Rotation of the filler and the electro-magnets operator on successive days. This would mean that the two men directly concerned with filling the moulds to the correct level and removing the separator grids the following day, would carry out both operations on the same batch of moulds.

3 Development of greater team capacity. The rate of production is controlled by the ease and speed with which the separator grid is removed from the mould. The analysis had shown that almost all the operators could influence this operation by the way they carried out their own task. The suggestion therefore was that all the operators, except the filler and the electro-magnets operator, should rotate jobs during an intensive learning period of one month, so that each could see how every job contributed to a successful production rate.

4 Introduction of a signal for moulds likely to stick. If the filler decided that a mould he had filled would stick for some reason, he should mark it with chalk so that the fork-lift driver could stack it separately from the rest, rather than, under the existing system, bringing it back to the line the following morning, where it would hold up production before being discarded as a "sticker."

There were also a number of minor proposals for changes in the technical system, of which an example was:

5 Addition of a white colouring agent to the mould release agent to make it easier for the filler to fill the mould to the correct level.

The department manager considered all the proposals for changing the social system were feasible and well worth a trial. He also favoured the idea of a white colouring agent. Unfortunately, however, he was posted overseas at about the time the study was completed. His successor was not as favourably inclined to the proposed changes and, as a relative newcomer to the department, he decided not to experiment with them. The opportunity of testing the extent to which the use of the analytical method might have contributed to an improved level of production on the unit was thus lost.

THE ROLE ANALYSIS METHOD

In parallel with the method of analysis described above, Tavistock and ERP were developing a method of analysing administrative or service departments which had no clearly defined technical system. This second method was less complex than the first but was also more tentative and untried in practice. It contained seven steps, which are summarised below. A more detailed description is given in Appendix 6.

1   Initial scanning. As for the other method, obtaining a general overview of the department to be analysed.

2   Objectives of the department. Defining objectives clearly and specifically, so that all activities in the department can be judged against them. This involves an analysis of all inputs to and outputs from the department and of all the steps taken to transform inputs into outputs. Final outputs should indicate objectives, but there will be other objectives concerned with maintaining and developing the department's own assets, both human and material.

3   Analysis of roles. Defining objectives of individual roles, using the same procedure as in step 2. This process should start at the top with the manager's role and work downwards.

4   Measurement of roles against psychological needs. Obtaining the manager's and the men's own perceptions of how far their existing jobs meet psychological needs.

5   Grouping of roles. Identifying necessary job interaction links which may lead to ideas for a different grouping of roles.

6   Proposals for change. Gathering ideas for change into an action programme.

7   Management by objectives. Introducing a framework for management by objectives at department, section and role levels.

APPLYING ROLE ANALYSIS IN PRACTICE

In early 1968 a study was made at Stanlow of part of the personnel function, the personnel services department. It resulted in a number of changes which were considered by the people concerned to have been successful. A further study then took place in the catering department, using a modified form of the role analysis method. This also produced very satisfactory results.

Both departments were considered to be operating efficiently before the studies began. Both managers suggested their departments for study, therefore, not because they felt they had big problems to solve but because they were keen to see if improved levels of performance and morale could be achieved by this way of seeking implementation of the philosophy.

Because of the amount of detail which would be needed, a comprehensive account of these studies is not included here. An attempt is made, however, to give a general idea of the way in which they were carried out and the sort of changes they resulted in.

Personnel services department
The department was responsible for central records, employee facilities, welfare and the social and sports club. It had a staff of eighteen. An action group was formed to guide the project. It was made up of the department manager, a Tavistock and an ERP representative and two clerks elected to this role by their colleagues following an introductory meeting at which the purposes of the study were explained and discussed with all members of the department.

The analysis was concerned with discovering how appropriate the department's activities, its organisation and its use of people were to the effective achievement of its objectives. It was also concerned with testing whether the department's objectives were consistent with those of the personnel function as a whole and with company objectives.

It proved a valuable method of identifying fairly quickly where the means being used to achieve objectives were not the most appropriate ones and it also led to the reformulation of objectives in some cases. The study undoubtedly contributed to creating a more participative climate in the department. In all, some twenty-three changes were recommended and most of them were accepted and implemented. They ranged in significance from the elimination of the role of senior supervisor, which happened to be temporarily vacant at the time of the study,

K

to the signing of memoranda by the clerks who prepared them, rather than by their supervisor.

Catering department

This study was spread over the period September 1968 to February 1969. Some of the steps from the nine-step method were incorporated in the role analysis approach on which it was based. This was because the department had several similarities to a production unit: it transformed physical raw materials to end products which were programmed some days ahead, it had identifiable units of operation and its products which did not meet specifications were either disposed of as waste or recycled.

Again an action group was set up, consisting of the department manager, a supervisor, a leading assistant and three canteen assistants including one shop steward. The outside experts attached to the group were the Tavistock representative and a member of the Stanlow personnel department.

As there were 125 people in the department including a number of part-time women, great care was taken to ensure that they knew what the study was about and had an opportunity to contribute their own ideas. After initial discussions with the supervisors, therefore, there were meetings with all the leading assistants and canteen assistants in groups of about twenty-five.

With the help of the action group a questionnaire was devised to gather information on feelings and attitudes in the department and to test how far psychological needs were being met. The results of this survey indicated that in the view of the employees, their major problems were not related to the nature of their work, but rather to communication barriers between some units and a somewhat inhibiting social climate in the department. It was therefore decided to invite the leading assistants to a weekend training course, held in the company hostel. Chefs and supervisors also attended. The programme was designed to:

1   Produce within the framework of the company philosophy a common understanding of departmental objectives
2   Break down unit and status barriers by getting people to work in pairs or groups
3   Give a better understanding of the principles of supervision through case study work
4   Give a better idea of the planning and control procedures in the department

5   Cause the leading assistants to give more thought to the needs of customers
6   Give some thought to future trends

The value of this training experience was very highly rated by the participants. It served as a demonstration of what could be achieved in freeing communications and in improving the social climate in the department.

During the course of the study, about fifty suggestions for change were put forward by the employees. Most of them were concerned with relatively minor adjustments to the technical system. Nevertheless, they were constructive and many of them served to make it easier for the job to be carried out effectively. About three-quarters of the suggestions were put into effect; where they were not, an explanation was given by the manager.

Conclusions
Evaluation of the results of projects such as these must necessarily be rather generalised: with so many different variables bearing on the activities of a department over a period of time, it is not possible to establish a quantifiable link between cause and effect.

Nevertheless, there is evidence which indicates that the catering department study produced favourable and lasting effects. For example, the level of seasonally adjusted absenteeism among canteen assistants went down during the study and remained down afterwards. It can be assumed that this was a result of the improved climate and of the discussions on absenteeism which took place during the departmental meetings, which led to a greater understanding of the problems created by absenteeism for those still at work.

Economic measures of the department's efficiency, such as the ratio of the cost of meals to the cash received, were improving before the study and continued to improve after it.

In April 1969 and January 1970 two different people who knew about the project but had not been involved in it conducted some random interviews with a number of employees in the catering department. Both sets of interviews indicated that the study was perceived to have had a considerable impact on the life of the department and that the general climate and employee morale was much improved. Two quotations from the interviews are typical of many:

"The general atmosphere here is completely different now. I really like coming to work now, not like before, when you felt you didn't matter as a human being."

"The place is much more organised and runs smoother. We have better equipment to work with now and last minute rushes seem easier to cope with somehow."

Certainly both analytical methods had demonstrated that they were very promising ways of applying the principle of joint optimisation and of achieving organisational improvements. A vital factor which they shared in common was the involvement of employees at all levels in the department under study both in the analytical process and in the development of an action programme. Unlike many organisational changes imposed from above, these self-generated change programmes tend to receive the full support and commitment of those who have helped to create them.

Chapter 13

Teesport: The Philosophy in Action

During the period when ERP was developing its ideas about a long-term plan, the company was designing a major new refinery to be constructed on Teesside. With a planned throughput of six million tons per annum, Teesport was to be an important addition to the company's refining capacity.

Features of the design were a highly integrated plant layout, with a central control room covering all the units; and a computer installation capable of monitoring and possibly later controlling a large percentage of the actual process operations. Unlike Shell Haven and Stanlow, Teesport was not to be a balancing refinery, so that its operations would be less complex and more stable than theirs. Because of these features, it was envisaged that the whole refinery could be operated with a very small number of operators on each shift.

Since it was planned that the operators would be able to cope with minor running maintenance work on the plants, and since major maintenance during shutdowns would in any event have to be handled by contract labour, it was decided to contract out all maintenance work to an engineering concern in the locality so that there were no engineering craftsmen on the refinery payroll.

Site preparation for the new refinery started in early 1965 and it came on stream, after considerable delays in construction, in April 1968.

DESIGN OF SOCIAL SYSTEM

As a new refinery on a green field site, Teesport clearly offered a great

135

opportunity not only to put into practice the ideas of the philosophy statement concerning job design, but also to establish a set of working conditions and practices which could serve as a model for the older refineries to try to follow.

The extent to which this opportunity was seized would depend, of course, on the Teesport management. The key people were all enthusiastic supporters of the philosophy concepts, and were committed to designing, and bringing into being, a social system which would match the technical system—with its novel features—in the best possible way.

The project manager, responsible for the construction and bringing on stream of the refinery, was a member of the first management conference at Selsdon Park in October 1965. So was the general manager, who would take over responsibility for running the refinery in 1968, and who had previously been deputy general manager at Stanlow. Other key people who had also come from Stanlow were the refinery superintendent, the technologist who worked on the computer programme, and the personnel adviser.

In 1964, ERP had drafted a set of personnel policies for Teesport, which were consistent with the ideal set of terms and conditions of employment which they envisaged as the target for the older refineries. During 1965, when the social system was being devised, in addition to Teesport's contacts with personnel people at head office on staffing, training and industrial relations matters, they also maintained a close liaison with ERP, who served, as it were, as a sounding-board for their ideas.

In December 1965, for example, a meeting was arranged at which the refinery superintendent outlined his proposals for manning the refinery to Tavistock and ERP. The meeting showed that the concept of joint optimisation had been deliberately taken into account and had had a considerable influence on the design of the social system. It also demonstrated that Teesport had moved a long way away from some tentative guidelines which had been formulated by the management in head office in early 1964, and which were characterised by the traditional emphasis on optimising the technical system at minimum cost, with little regard to the needs of the social system.

After the refinery came on stream in 1968, the Teesport organisation proved very successful, with an unusually high level of commitment to refinery objectives at all levels. One reason for this success was undoubtedly the amount of care taken over the design of the organisation and the training of the staff. By late 1969, however, certain difficulties had begun to emerge. The remainder of this chapter will describe some of the features of the original social system which were new and different. It will then consider some of the problems which have emerged and the changes in the social system which they have occasioned.

ROLE OF SUPERVISORS AND OPERATORS

Since Teesport wanted to create roles both for supervisors and operators which would be demanding and challenging, and as they were determined to break away from the established patterns of the older refineries, they decided to eliminate some of the traditional levels from their organisation structure. Thus the operators, who would be highly flexible and skilled men, would report direct to a shift supervisor, with no intervening chargehand or foreman. The supervisors would report direct to the head of operations. The line of command from refinery manager to the shift operators manning the plant would consist of only four communication steps compared with the six or seven steps in the older refineries.

Great care was taken to select people who would be capable of filling these roles and who were sympathetic to the concepts of flexibility and challenge which Teesport planned to build into their organisation. The first step was to select the five supervisors who would be responsible for running the shift teams of operators. All five came from other Shell refineries and joined Teesport in March 1966. The refinery superintendent's idea was that after a period devoted to their own training, the supervisors would themselves play an important role in the selection and training of their own teams of operators, and indeed would be fully involved in all matters affecting the building up of the organisation.

The time between March 1966 and the start up in early 1968, was longer than originally envisaged, owing to construction delays, but it is interesting that everyone concerned was convinced that this period of training and preparation was invaluable and not a bit too long.

After initial training at Teesport the five supervisors spent six weeks with the refinery superintendent at Shell's Oakville refinery outside Toronto in Canada, where they underwent further training. The reason for this was that Oakville was similar in many respects to what Teesport would be: it had, for example, a compact and integrated design layout, and utilised up-to-date ideas on operator flexibility; it had a similarly high level of capital intensity; and it contracted out all maintenance work.

On their return to Teesport, the supervisors prepared to assist with the recruitment and training of the operators. This involved coaching—by the training adviser—in methods and techniques for interviewing candidates, and for training the recruits. In the meantime, they also took a hand in such matters as the final formulation of personnel policies, the layout of the control room building, the preparation of an information handbook and the final stages of the drafting of the trade union agreement which would cover the operators.

The refinery was to be manned by twenty-nine operators on each shift, so that there were a total of 116 jobs on the four shifts. In addition, since the intention was to run the refinery without overtime, forty more men were needed to provide cover for all kinds of absence, holidays, and time spent away from the job on training. Thus a total of 156 men had to be recruited.

The supervisors decided on the wording of the advertisements for operating staff which appeared in the local press. For the 156 jobs available over 3000 men applied. The letter which invited them to complete a formal application form concluded with the following paragraph: "We are now recruiting operating staff who will be trained on site for approximately six months. No one should under-estimate the difficulties that are bound to arise in starting up a refinery of this complexity. We are seeking men who will accept the challenge of these difficulties and who will prove to be adaptable to changing circumstances. We shall depend a great deal upon the individual effort and sense of responsibility of each member of the staff, who will—after training—be required to work without close supervision." An intensive interviewing programme was set up and the supervisors were part of the interviewing team. An important element in the process was to obtain from the applicants at their first interview their reactions to the sort of responsible, flexible jobs which were envisaged for operators, so that people to whom this did not appeal could withdraw from the follow-up interview.

Once the teams were recruited, each supervisor assumed responsibility for training his own team, under the general guidance of the training adviser. They did, of course, get assistance from other members of the staff who gave lectures on specialised subjects. Practical training on operations and maintenance was interspersed with theoretical sessions. Aids to training included a complete scale model of the process units and a control panel simulator on which operating techniques could be practised.

During this period of training, the supervisors conducted sessions with their teams on the company philosophy statement. The concepts of joint optimisation, and of meeting people's psychological needs, had particular relevance at Teesport, where the whole refinery was to be manned by only twenty-nine operators during any one shift. The need to make the best use of the men's capabilities, and the wish to design challenging jobs, were mutually supporting.

Also vital was the need to develop the operators' capabilities to handle information quickly and effectively. Already identified as the critical human requirement for control of a refinery operating system, information handling was particularly important at Teesport, with its very high level of instrumentation and automation. Any failure or mal-function of the automatic control system would mean that the operator had to take over control himself, knowing that delay was likely to be costly. Some of the implications of this man-machine relationship are examined in the next section.

The payment structure for the operators was fitted to the needs of the system. As it was essential that each operator should be highly flexible, and capable of operating a number of different units, the level of salary was geared not to the specific job he was on but to the extent he had developed and proved his capability to run a number of different jobs. It was envisaged that each operator could learn up to seven different jobs. After training and experience on each job, he would be given a written and verbal test by the shift supervisor. As his range of competence was widened in this way, his salary rate was increased accordingly.

Also essential was the employment of sufficient spare operators, to enable the work to be covered whilst a process of continual training was maintained. In keeping with the general philosophy, it was agreed that each team of operators would handle its own relief arrangements for covering absences of any kind.

The effect of involving the supervisors from the outset in matters which would vitally influence the running of the refinery, and the building of responsible, flexible and challenging jobs for supervisors and operators, was to create in both groups a very high level of commitment to their tasks and to achieving refinery objectives.

Evidence of this commitment is provided by the fact that in the period of over twelve months between the recruitment of the 156 operators, and the start up of the refinery in 1968, only five of these men resigned. This represented an extremely low turnover rate of a little over 3 per cent a year. Wastage would increase later, as the operators found that their training had fitted them for more lucrative jobs overseas.

So far as the supervisors were concerned, one of them has commented on his own reaction to this period of time in the following terms: "Everyone contributed, it was a wonderful experience and I hope that the marvellous spirit of Teesport today lives on."

OPTIMISING THE COMPUTER–OPERATOR RELATIONSHIP

Mention has already been made of the computer installed in Teesport's centralised control room, which could carry out much of the data-logging and plant control operations normally done by operators in the older established refineries.

The refinery superintendent, who was concerned with the design of the operator role, and the technologist responsible for the computer programme, both saw the computer–operator interface as a critical factor for the effective operation of the refinery. Both saw it as essential that the way the interface was set up should be governed by the concept of joint optimisation, by making the best match between the capabilities of the man and the machine.

One choice available to them was to maximise the use of the computer's capabilities: in other words, to close as many information and control loops as possible, so that the need for intervention by the operator was reduced to a minimum. Whilst such a choice may well have been attractive from a purely technical point of view, the Teesport people were concerned about its implications for the role of the operator. If his role was to be confined largely to monitoring the performance of the computer, this would neither be sufficiently challenging, nor involve him sufficiently in the on-going process of control to enable him at any time quickly and effectively to assume manual control in the event of a breakdown of the computer. Yet it was essential that he should be able to do so, since delay or mistakes could be very costly.

They decided therefore that a balance had to be struck between what was technically feasible, on the one hand, and what was necessary, on the other, to create a role for the operator that would enable him to become internally motivated to perform his task effectively. This meant that certain loops which could technically have been closed, were passed instead, as it were, through the operator, so that he could exert his influence and become part of the control process. The role of the computer was accordingly seen as the logging of data, the automatic control of certain variables, and the rapid provision of information on which the operator or supervisor could take better decisions about the control of other process variables.

The setting up of the computer–operator interface does therefore give an excellent practical illustration of applying the concept of joint optimisation. Rather than maximising the technical use of the computer at the expense of the operator's role, the contribution of both was balanced in a way which would ensure a more effective performance in the long term.

TERMS AND CONDITIONS OF WORK

Another significant achievement at Teesport was the establishment of a set of working conditions and terms of employment which were quite different from the traditions of the older refineries in the company. All the features which it was hoped would eventually be introduced at the older refineries through productivity bargaining were incorporated in the Teesport system from the outset.

Whilst clearly it was less difficult in some ways to set up a new system on a green field site than to change long established systems at older sites, Teesport was also faced with serious problems to overcome. At the time they decided to approach the TGWU about an agreement to cover the operators, there was still in existence a national TGWU agreement with the company, laying down common conditions for all the existing refineries. Furthermore, the overwhelming pattern of custom and practice in the heavily industrialised Teesside area was similar to that of the company's older refineries, and quite different, therefore, from the new pattern Teesport wanted to establish. Some advisers argued moreover that the unions in the area would be very resistant to changes in the normal pattern and that it would be wiser, therefore, to conform.

Teesport, however, saw it as essential that the terms and conditions of work should be consistent with the philosophy which had guided the way people's roles had been set up. They were determined that all employees at Teesport would be members of the staff: there would be no hourly paid employees and no time clocks. Everyone would receive an annual salary, paid monthly into his bank account. There would be no provision for extra payments for overtime. All staff below management level would be compensated for overtime by corresponding time off. Everyone would enjoy the same set of sickness benefits and pension fund arrangements. Everyone would share the same restaurant, although the shift operators would normally eat in the mess-room on the process units.

Rather than await an approach from the union, they decided to take the initiative by contacting the local TGWU officials well before the recruitment of operators was started. After discussions between head office and national officials in London had cleared the way, Teesport talked with the local officials. They were entirely open about their intentions, and their wish to negotiate a separate and completely different agreement from the existing national one. The union officials, far from justifying the warning mentioned above, proved receptive to Teesport's ideas and contributed in joint discussions to their development. The outcome was an agreement covering the operating staff which embraced virtually everything Teesport would have wished. Both sides recognised the experimental nature of the agreement and accepted that changes might be needed in the future.

Undoubtedly, therefore, Teesport had succeeded in setting up a new organisation which was a practical demonstration of the value of the two lines of action embodied in the company development programme: the creation of commitment to tasks and objectives through appropriate job design; and the establishment of appropriate terms and conditions of employment.

The concluding section of this chapter will describe some of the problems which have faced Teesport since the start up and the effect they have had upon the organisation.

ORGANISATION PROBLEMS

No matter how well designed, no organisation is perfect nor can it hope to remain static. On the contrary it is a feature of an effective organisation that it is able to adapt to changing conditions whether these arise internally or in the outside environment.

Furthermore, it seems inevitable that any organisation which sets out to innovate and starts carrying out its activities in ways which strike others as different and perhaps risky will be subject to quite strong pressures to regress and conform to the conventional norm.

At Teesport a number of factors have combined to bring about two significant changes in the original design of the social system. First, the amount of supervision has been considerably increased with the introduction of an additional level of communication—assistant supervisors—between the operators and the original shift supervisors who have been reclassified as shift managers. Second, the span of potential job flexibility among the operators has been reduced from a maximum of seven different jobs to qualify for the top salary rate to four.

The internal factors which contributed to these changes were:

1 Since before the start up in 1968 the refinery suffered a succession of technical faults and problems which imposed a high level of disturbance on the engineering and technical staff at all levels, including the process operators. This situation tended to prevent the establishment of steady state operation which had been the basis for the original job design and induced a certain amount of unexpected stress in the social system.

2 After the start up the work load of the refinery expanded because, for example, of the taking over of rail marshalling activities from the railway employees.

3 Not surprisingly the turnover of operators did not remain at the initial abnormally low level of a little over 3 per cent a year. After the start up in 1968, turnover climbed to an average of about 10 per cent a year, mainly because of operators taking up jobs in overseas refineries. Whilst this is still not a high level it increased the number of new operators who had to be recruited into the Teesport system.

4 The combined effect of the increase in the number of operators to handle the greater work load, the promotion of some twelve operators to the role of assistant supervisor and the replacement of 10 per cent annual wastage, was to dilute quite severely the original work force with new recruits. This posed a considerable training problem since Teesport was faced with the need to train the new recruits under difficult operational conditions to the same high level achieved with the original men before start up.

5 Practical experience of operating the system led Teesport to the view that the original range of flexibility envisaged for the operators was too wide and caused too much movement between different jobs and too little continuity on the units. It was also considered necessary to strengthen the supervisory structure because of the difficulties mentioned above and the complexity of the task.

Certain external pressures made themselves felt and also tended to influence Teesport to move back towards a more conventional organisational pattern. For example:

1 The loading of rail cars at Teesport involves three different jobs:

(a) The operation of a computer which controls the actual filling operation and prints out the appropriate invoice.

(b) The role of filler which involves lining up the rail car under the filling head and, after filling, closing down the loading hatch.

(c) The floor man role, responsible for the general cleanliness of the filling area.

Whereas in other locations it was normal for a staff grade man to handle the computer operation and operators to look after the other two jobs, it was a feature of the Teesport system that the operators handled all three roles, rotating around the tasks in a cycle which they themselves determined. This system worked very successfully. One day, however, there was a fire many miles from Teesport resulting from an oil spillage on one of these rail cars. Although there was no concrete evidence it was judged that the fire had been because of the failure to fasten down securely the rail car loading hatch. The effect of this incident was to create strong pressures to introduce a supervisor who would be responsible for the safety of the filling operation.

2   Ships' officers loading at refinery jetties are accustomed to exchanging the necessary documentation with a white collar supervisor. At Teesport the jetty operator was responsible for carrying out the loading operation, completing the loading documentation and handing this over to the ship's officer. This change in normal practice also gave rise to pressures to appoint a supervisor to deal with the documentation side of the job.

3   When Teesport started up, its terms and conditions of employment and job structuring were sufficiently different from the norm that it seemed appropriate to look upon it as a separate and distinctive organisation. Since then, however, changes through productivity type bargaining in other organisations have tended to bring their terms and conditions of employment—such as annual salary and staff status— closer to those of Teesport without, however, approaching the level of job flexibility and responsibility achieved at Teesport. The effect of this partial closing of the gap has been to create pressure to close it further by moving the Teesport job structuring back towards the conventional norm.

It is too early to judge how Teesport will deal with the sort of problems outlined above, and impossible to guess what new problems the future may bring. It will, however, be interesting to see whether the organisation which so successfully met its initial objective to build an effective and highly motivated system, will be as successful in adapting to the changes and problems which have faced it since it came on stream.

Part Five
EFFECT ON
PRODUCTIVITY BARGAINING

L

Chapter 14

Preparing the Ground

This chapter and the next are concerned with the second major area of action agreed in 1965: namely the preparation for productivity bargaining with the unions and the negotiation of new agreements which would incorporate radical changes in the terms and conditions of employment of unionised employees.

As described in Chapter 4, this activity was to be conducted in parallel with the philosophy dissemination programme. It was hoped that the results of the productivity bargaining would clear the ground of restrictive practices, thus making it easier to introduce new methods of work and to redesign jobs, in line with the intention of the philosophy statement.

The securing of successful agreements with the unions was important in its own right, of course. Many people believed, however, that little of real value in this area could be achieved without a significant change of attitude on the part of the hourly paid employees. The concluding of satisfactory bargains was therefore seen as an important criterion of success for the whole of the philosophy programme.

It is not proposed to discuss in any detail the mechanics of the productivity bargaining, since these have been well documented elsewhere (North and Buckingham, 1969). There were, however, certain novel features which are worth recording, since they undoubtedly contributed to the success of the final outcome. During the preparatory stage, there were two such features: the study teams, and the joint working parties.

STUDY TEAMS

The idea of setting up a small *ad hoc* team to carry out a special study or project is not of course new. What was a novel feature of this bargaining effort was the establishment of a set of interrelated teams who were briefed to carry out a co-ordinated study in depth of the whole field likely to be affected by the eventual productivity bargains.

As the result of the teams' work, the company obtained a valuable set of objective data on the implications of any of the changes likely to emerge during the bargaining process. These data were very helpful in setting parameters for change (for example, how much intercraft flexibility was practicable and desirable) and were available when required to the people involved in the negotiation of the new agreements.

The areas covered by the teams are described below: it will be seen that some closely interlinked areas were dealt with in sequence by the same team.

Team 1 (One engineer, one technologist, one personnel man)
>   (a) *Overtime situation.* The factors contributing to current overtime levels. Methods by which overtime could be reduced or eliminated
>   (b) *Job flexibility.* The extent of intercraft and operator-craft flexibility (or work-sharing) which it was realistic to aim for, and would be practicable to implement. What the training requirements would be
>   (c) *Time flexibility.* The extent of temporary shift working and staggered day working which would be required to enable all planned work to be carried out without the need for overtime

Team 2 (Two personnel men)
>   (a) *Wage and salary structure.* The factors involved in, and the implications of introducing an annual salary for existing hourly paid employees
>   (b) *Single status.* The implications of introducing staff status for existing hourly paid employees, including the effect upon existing staff groups
>   (c) *Contractors.* The effects of all the above matters upon the employment on the refinery sites of contractors' hourly paid employees

Team 3 (Two engineers)
>   *Time standards for maintenance work*

Team 4 (Two technologists, one economist, one accountant)

Yardsticks of operating performance, at company, refinery, and plant levels

These last two areas for study had arisen independently of the productivity bargaining exercise, but both had relevance to it. They reflected the need, which had been highlighted in the dissemination conferences, for more effective ways of measuring the efficiency of maintenance and operating work, and of judging the value of changes which might be introduced.

JOINT WORKING PARTIES

It had always been envisaged that after the study teams had completed their work, there would be some form of joint discussion with the unions in order to arrive at a new set of agreements. Certainly the company did not wish to place a detailed plan on the negotiating table. But the machinery for the joint development of a plan had not been specified. It was during the life of the study teams, in early 1966, when the dissemination conferences were under way, that the idea of joint working parties (JWPs) first emerged.

The JWPs were to be a completely new departure. They were to bring together representatives of management and shop stewards, not in the usual bargaining frame of reference, but in a new collaborative problem-solving frame of reference. They would sit, as it were, around the table together, rather than facing each other across it.

Their terms of reference would be to consider how to remove impediments to efficiency; and to work out what, in their joint view, would be the most appropriate set of terms and conditions of work for the existing hourly paid employees. This was to be done without any regard to the price of whatever they might agree was needed. Thus they might recommend that hourly paid employees should be paid on the basis of an annual salary: but it was outside their terms of reference to discuss how much that salary should be.

The intention was that when the JWPs had reached agreement on what they considered should form the contents of a productivity deal, they would jointly recommend their proposals to the management and to the unions, so that negotiations could be carried out through the normal channels. Neither the management, nor the unions, however, would be in any way committed to what their representatives had said in the JWPs, nor bound to accept any of their recommendations. This meant that the members of the JWPs were completely free of any negotiating responsibility and could develop their ideas freely, without fear of the consequences.

The company would have preferred that one common JWP could have been set up at each refinery, in which shop steward representatives of both craftsmen and operators could have been included. This would, in theory, have made possible the development of identical proposals for negotiation with the craft unions and the TGWU respectively. In practice, however, this was achieved only at Ardrossan refinery. At both Shell Haven and Stanlow, the craftsmen and the operators insisted on their own separate JWPs. It will be recalled that the shop stewards at Stanlow proposed a common JWP for crafts and operators at their first philosophy conference. This proposal was not ratified by the union membership, nor by the union officials.

The JWP structure at the two major refineries was therefore, from the outset, a complicated one. The key JWPs were the two at each refinery covering craftsmen and operators, since it was in the agreements affecting these two groups that the most radical changes were hoped for. Also important, however, were JWPs set up with representatives of unionised laboratory staff, since it was hoped to agree a productivity deal with the union concerned, USDAW; and with supervisory staff, so that they too would discuss with management representatives the contributions they could themselves make towards increased productivity.

The remainder of this chapter will describe some of the difficulties which arose as the result of setting up the JWPs, and some of the positive results they achieved. To avoid undue complexity the account will concentrate on the key groups only.

JOINT WORKING PARTY DIFFICULTIES

A number of difficulties beset the functioning of the JWPs. Whilst some of them had perhaps been foreseen, all of them had been under-estimated.

New frame of reference

It was not at all easy for the members—management representatives or shop stewards—to make the change from a bargaining to a collaborative frame of reference. In most cases, this simply involved some delay before the JWPs were able to get down to their real business. In the case of the craft JWP at Shell Haven, however, it resulted in the winding up of the group fairly soon after it had started. This was the inevitable outcome when the shop steward members made it clear that they did not intend to change their frame of reference. They were undoubtedly suspicious of the company's intentions and they accordingly insisted that before there could be any joint discussion of change, the management would have to agree not only that no one would lose his job as a direct result of any changes discussed, but also that a guaranteed level of salary should be established as a base line whatever the final outcome might be. Whilst the point about security of employment was acceptable to the management, the demand concerning a guaranteed salary level was directly contrary to the purpose of the JWP, and left no alternative to winding it up prematurely.

Communications
Once the remaining JWPs began serious discussion about the sort of changes that might be included in a productivity plan, it became apparent that they were losing the support and the trust of the mass of the shop-floor people whom they represented. Rumours began to circulate around the refineries, unrest followed. It was clear that something had to be done to ensure that the shop floor received rapid and accurate information about what was going on in the JWPs.

Another aspect of this problem was the relationship between the shop steward members of the groups, and their own union officials. Here, too, normal channels of communication seemed inadequate, and some officials became worried that their stewards would go too far in agreeing proposals which looked like concessions to the company.

It became necessary, therefore, to set up an elaborate network of communications at each refinery. These included arrangements for the shop stewards to make verbal on-site reports on progress to the people they represented; the establishment of a bridging committee to bring together representatives from the different JWPs, and a comprehensive system of written summaries, which were widely distributed, including copies to the union officials.

Impact of outside events
On several occasions the work of some of the JWPs was set back by disagreements or conflict which, although not directly relevant to the JWPs' activities, resulted in the unions withdrawing their shop stewards from the discussions. It seemed that a few union officials,

perceiving the importance the company attached to the work of the JWPs, saw the temporary withdrawal of their stewards' co-operation as an effective, cheap, and easily applied sanction at their disposal. A major disruption affecting the craft JWP at Stanlow was a strike of craftsmen in April 1967, on the issue of unionisation of craft foremen. It was noteworthy, however, that after the strike was over, the JWP in due course began to function again.

Complexity of the task

The JWPs had a complex set of issues to discuss. Some of them found it necessary to set up small sub-groups from among their members to work full-time on a particular problem. Some issues affected more than one JWP, such as the question of work sharing between craftsmen and operators. Besides this complexity, there was the burden of keeping the special communication network functioning effectively; and this, together with the growing pressure from the shop floor for some settlement, after a long period without a wage increase, eventually led to all the JWPs being discontinued before any of them had completed their tasks.

In spite of this, their efforts were far from wasted. Their detailed discussions of all the major relevant proposals for change and their efforts to keep everyone on the refinery fully informed about the progress they were making undoubtedly contributed a great deal to the eventual success of the productivity bargains. The pattern they had set of really effective consultation and communication, was to carry over into the bargaining phase. Never before in the company had people at all levels been so well briefed on the changes which were likely to be introduced in the union agreements, and on their implications.

JOINT WORKING PARTY ACHIEVEMENTS

The notion of setting up JWPs had been seen as entirely consistent with the style of management reflected in the philosophy statement. It was a mechanism for enabling the people who would be directly affected by changes in working practices to contribute their own knowledge and ideas to the formulation of those changes. It was to be hoped that by this means, not only would a better set of change proposals emerge as the result of the shop stewards' participation, but that the shop stewards and their colleagues would be more committed to their successful introduction than if they had had no part in their formulation.

Although the JWPs did not fully meet their objectives, they did achieve some notable specific successes. Examples of these are described in the remainder of this chapter.

At *Ardrossan*, the JWP was unique in that it included representatives from all three unionised groups: craftsmen, operators, and laboratory staff. Discussions made good progress from the start, and led for example to two specific proposals, both of which the members were willing to have implemented before the negotiation of a formal productivity agreement.

The first proposal was for the introduction of continuous shift coverage in the refinery's installation department, which would eliminate the need for the excessive overtime which some individuals had to work under the previous day-work system. This change was put into effect and meant that the new system had the potential to cope with future increases in output without increased manpower costs.

The second proposal was to eliminate all overtime payments to employees covered by the TGWU agreement, and to compensate them instead with appropriate time off. Whilst this proposal was entirely in line with the company's own wishes, it could not be implemented in isolation at Ardrossan, since at that time the national agreement with the TGWU was still in force, and Ardrossan had to conform to its stipulations. This situation did therefore lend weight to the company's wish to replace the national agreement with separate agreements at each refinery, so that each could make progress at its own pace, and in a direction which suited best its own particular circumstances.

At *Stanlow*, after some time spent in getting used to the collaborative style, both the craft and the operator JWPs made good early progress in their discussions. Agenda lists of all relevant points for discussion were drawn up and were worked through in considerable detail.

Both groups agreed in principle with the notion that remuneration should be based on an annual salary, and that overtime payments should be eliminated. Both agreed that if such a system were to function effectively, it would be necessary to reduce the actual need for overtime to be worked, and that this required greater job flexibility and time flexibility. An early suggestion about time flexibility from a craft shop steward JWP member was, for example, that craftsmen should make themselves available to work any 160 hours in every four-week period, thus allowing virtually complete flexibility in work planning. This particular suggestion did not survive the test of further discussion, but it is significant that the shop steward felt free to put forward so radical an idea.

The operator JWP was also concerned with the implications of ceasing payments for overtime. All its members agreed that whilst time and job flexibility would help to reduce the need for overtime to a minimum, there would inevitably be occasions when unforeseen work would have to be covered by overtime. It was agreed, moreover, that in such circumstances, management would need to be able to rely on people being willing to work overtime: in other words, overtime would cease to be voluntary and employees would have to give up their right to refuse it.

This led the JWP on to a discussion of how to limit within reasonable bounds the amount of disturbance to which any individual could be submitted by being required to work obligatory overtime, for which he would not be paid (but would get compensatory time off). The outcome was a jointly agreed set of constraints, which would prevent any individual being exposed to undue disturbance. This agreement was in due course incorporated in the formal productivity bargain negotiated with the union.

A further development was that the shop steward members of the JWP worked out a sophisticated decision-tree model to show how, in various orders of priority, planned or unplanned absences of operators would be covered on the process units. This was to lead to agreement that the team of operators on each unit would assume responsibility for organising all their own cover for leave or absence, and that the supervisor would be involved only if they had a problem they could not solve.

At *Shell Haven*, there was, in the operator JWP, a dramatic example of changed attitudes among the shop steward representatives. In previous years, these TGWU shop stewards had been known for their determined opposition to any reduction in the number of operators manning a unit, even where technical advances had clearly reduced the work load. Many a long hour of negotiation had been spent by management representatives, arguing such issues with them and their union official, in a traditional bargaining "win—lose" frame of reference.

These same shop stewards had now enthusiastically accepted the company's philosophy statement and had entered into the JWP discussions in a truly collaborative frame of reference. This was the more significant since, it will be recalled, the senior craft shop stewards at Shell Haven had rejected the philosophy statement and were to refuse to collaborate in their JWP.

Early in 1967 the TGWU shop stewards put forward a suggestion in their JWP that was to lead to what became known as the "East Site experiment." Their proposal was that a part of the refinery—the East Site—should be operated for a period on experimental lines which would demonstrate how new and more flexible methods of working could eliminate the need for overtime, and could enable the units to be run with a 10 per cent reduction in the number of operators.

The means of achieving these ambitious targets were to be greater job flexibility and time flexibility. The process units on the East Site would be regrouped into four blocks, and the operators would work flexibly anywhere within their own block, thus becoming, in effect, a block team. Additional training would be required to equip them to do this, and the result would be to extend their skills and knowledge, and thus to make better use of their capabilities.

So far as time flexibility was concerned, the operators themselves devised new shift cycles which would make it possible for certain tasks, which had previously necesssitated a considerable amount of overtime, to be done within the revised basic shift hours.

This proposal was developed in detail by the JWP, in collaboration with the East Site department managers and supervisors concerned, and the experiment was launched in June 1967. It was to run for six months, and there was no commitment binding either party to extend it in time, or to spread it to other parts of the refinery. The JWP discussed at length the implications of the experiment on the earnings of the operators involved. An arrangement was eventually agreed which in effect meant that the operators would continue to receive approximately the average of their previous earnings, although those who had always worked a lot of overtime, would now receive reduced earnings.

Of the ten operators who represented the 10 per cent reduction in operating manpower, three became additional spare operators, to permit extra training to take place, and the other seven were redeployed in other parts of the refinery.

The experiment worked well. Although some practical difficulties arose, particularly because of insufficient training opportunities for the operators, it was judged an undoubted success. The units were operated efficiently with the smaller work force, and overtime, whilst not eliminated, was very much reduced. Although in some cases, operators did not take kindly to having to share with others responsibility for a job which had been their own for a number of years, the majority felt that the opportunities for learning and doing different jobs was a rewarding experience.

At the end of the six months' trial period, however, the experiment was stopped. There was no sign yet of a productivity deal ready for negotiation, and the union members elected that the East Site should revert to its previous method of operation. Although this was disappointing, the East Site experiment had served a very useful purpose, and the lessons it had taught were not to be wasted. The same block team concept of running process units would be built into the eventual refinery-wide agreement with the union.

A further idea to emerge from the experiment was a proposal made by the senior shop steward who had played a major part in getting the experiment under way. He suggested that during the period of radical changes in practice which the experiment involved, it would have been helpful to have had someone from the JWP available who could have quickly resolved difficulties arising from some people's lack of knowledge of the exact terms and conditions agreed for the period of the experiment.

This idea was to be developed by Shell Haven and incorporated in their productivity bargaining process with the TGWU. This is described in the next chapter.

Chapter 15

Results of Productivity Bargaining

When the various JWPs were wound up in 1967, without having produced a plan which they could jointly recommend, it fell to the management representatives to produce specific proposals as a basis of negotiations with the unions. The plans which they produced naturally reflected in very large measure the work which had been done in the JWPs.

The negotiating procedure was itself somewhat complicated. There were several phases to be worked through. After reaching agreement on the form and content of the new agreements, there was lengthy negotiation on the level of annual salary to be paid. The bargain had then to be submitted to the Department of Employment and Productivity for approval, since at that time the UK incomes policy specified that wage increases above a certain level could be given only in cases where they were justified by acceptance of changes that would lead to higher productivity. Finally, there had to be a "lead-in" period, during which the changes in work practices could be gradually brought into effect, and the necessary training carried out.

The road to the eventual productivity bargains was therefore long and hard. The JWPs had been set up during the second half of 1966. The first productivity bargain was not struck until May 1968, at Ardrossan. At Stanlow, the new agreement with the craft unions became effective in January 1969, and that with the TGWU in September 1969. At Shell Haven, the new TGWU agreement took effect in October 1969, after a four-month lead-in period, but the craft agreement was not effective until November 1970. This long delay in reaching agreement with the craft unions at Shell Haven was due partly, it must be assumed, to the lack of progress made in the craft JWP before it was wound up. There were also delays and complications in the actual negotiations with the unions, which started in February 1969, included what was termed a "mini-deal" in 1969, and finally achieved a full productivity bargain in late 1970.

The time and effort devoted to the process of negotiation across the company were an indication of the management's determination that however radical the changes agreed with the unions might be, they would also be realistic, and would in fact be put into practice in the work situation.

It was not unknown in the UK industrial scene for apparently successful productivity bargains to be negotiated in good faith with union officials, but to fail absolutely when it came to putting them into effect on the shop floor. Such failure could be caused by the impracticability of changes agreed to on paper, a lack of commitment on the part of supervisors, or simply the unwillingness of people on the shop floor to put into effect changes which they did not want, although these changes had been agreed and accepted on their behalf. It was to avoid this sort of failure that unprecedented efforts were made to ensure that people at all levels in the organisation knew exactly what the bargaining was about and what changes it would introduce.

BRIEFING SUPERVISORS

An example of the care taken to communicate the content of the new agreements to the supervisory staff who would be responsible for administering them on the job, can be quoted from Stanlow. In the early part of 1968, when discussions were under way with the unions, a series of twelve weekend conferences were arranged to cover all the refinery's supervisory staff.

The conferences were on a residential basis, following the pattern. established by the philosophy conferences, and using the same hotel. Their purpose was to work through in detail the change proposals under discussion and to help the supervisors explore the implications of these changes for their own roles and for the people they supervised. A second objective was to go over the main concepts of the philosophy statement again and to show how the productivity bargains fitted in to the wider programme of implementation measures then being developed.

Stanlow decided upon residential conferences for this purpose because they were convinced that the only really effective method of ensuring that complex matters and their implications were understood, was to give people the opportunity of discussing them and debating them over a reasonable period of time. They considered that the productivity bargains were sufficiently important to warrant this amount of time and effort. At each conference, some of the people involved in the negotiations with the unions were present, which made it possible for full and frank discussion of all the points at issue.

As an introduction to the working sessions on the proposed content of the new agreements, the supervisors were given a talk explaining the objectives of the event, and linking it to the need to make better use of human resources, and to develop people's capabilities, which was a fundamental part of the overall philosophy. The concluding paragraphs of that talk are reproduced below, since they give a good indication of the climate in which these conferences were conducted.

> Finally, there is the area of creating the conditions in which people can and want to use such skills as they possess or are capable of acquiring.
>
> The introduction of joint productivity planning did not spring directly from the philosophy conferences but it did spring from the same beliefs that gave rise to the philosophy document. This belief was that our human resources were not being efficiently utilised, and hence very often neither were our material resources. The thinking was that we could increase the efficient use of our employees by jointly discussing with them the ways and means of increasing their effectiveness. Hence the setting up of working parties not just of the unionised groups but also of supervisory staff. Hence the interlinking productivity proposals for monthly as well as hourly paid employees.
>
> The productivity proposals which have resulted from these joint discussions must therefore be seen as part of the overall plan to create the right kind of conditions where all employees are internally motivated towards achieving the company's primary objective.
>
> The philosophy is not productivity deals. Productivity bargaining must be seen in proper perspective. It is only one part, albeit an important one, of the company's effort to make the most efficient use of its human resources.

WHAT THE BARGAINS ACHIEVED

It is not proposed to attempt a comprehensive account of the outcome of the various productivity bargains. It is, however, relevant to see to what extent they fulfilled the broad expectations which the company had in mind when the study teams were set up in 1965. Whilst there were variations between the refinery agreements, and between the craft and operator agreements at each refinery, a successful outcome was achieved in four of the five main areas covered by the work of the study teams.

1   The elimination of overtime payments. This was achieved in all the agreements. At Shell Haven, and subsequently at Stanlow, payment of a social disturbance allowance was negotiated. This was a modest rate of allowance related not to overtime hours, but to the amount of time people might have to work outside the normal hours of day-work. The same rationale applied therefore to this allowance as to the payment of a shift allowance to shift workers: both constituted a compensation for the disturbance of working abnormal hours, and neither provided an incentive for working, or "manufacturing," overtime.

2   The establishment of an annual salary as the basis of payment for all employees. This was also achieved in all the agreements.

3   Extensions of job flexibility, both between crafts, and between craftsmen and operators. Significant improvements were made in this area.

4   Extensions of time flexibility. Significant improvements were also made here, making it more possible to schedule work to be carried out within people's normal basic forty-hour week.

It is clear, therefore, that the bulk of company expectations were indeed met. Whilst the improvements achieved may not of themselves increase the level of people's motivation, nor their commitment to objectives, they should certainly help to create a more appropriate work setting in which increased motivational levels can be hoped for through such measures as job enrichment or job redesign. The extension of work roles in order to utilise the newly agreed levels of job flexibility, will itself, of course, involve an element of job enrichment in some cases.

The other change originally envisaged as desirable, and examined by a study team, was the establishment of *single status for all employees*. This was not a feature of the bargaining, nor was it in fact an issue which was discussed formally with the unions. It was felt that, as the result of the changes noted above, and the elimination of all time-clocks, there were in practice very few remaining status distinctions between the staff and the employees who had previously been hourly paid. It was decided therefore not to pursue the matter further at this stage.

A few particular features of some of the bargains are described in the remainder of this chapter.

Ardrossan

As the smallest refinery, with a high level of morale and a tradition of good relationships at all levels within the location and with the unions, it was not perhaps surprising that Ardrossan was the first to conclude its productivity bargains. It will be recalled that even in early 1967, the willingness of TGWU members to eliminate overtime payments had emerged through the JWP discussions.

The new agreements contained provision for a high level of flexibility and interchangeability of personnel. The effects of such improvements are more easily identified in a small location, than in the very much more complex larger refineries. At Ardrossan, since the agreements came into effect in May 1968, it has been possible to cope with an approximately constant work load with an overall reduction of nearly 13 per cent in the number of employees. Furthermore, the annual refinery shutdown for maintenance in 1969 was completed with considerably fewer man hours of work, and with less expenditure on manpower costs than the equivalent shutdown in 1966. Even taking into consideration changes in the technology, the most important factor contributing to this significant improvement in performance, was the introduction of new working methods made possible in 1969 by the provision for increased flexibility and work sharing in the productivity agreements.

Stanlow

A notable feature of the Stanlow agreements was the integration of craftsmen into the operating teams on some of the process units. This meant that one of the original operators in the team would be replaced by a craftsman. He would function as an operator when circumstances on the unit demanded it, but would at other times carry out maintenance work on the unit. An additional advantage would be that the craftsman would be more closely identified with the maintenance problems of the unit, with added interest in his job.

M

The process of growing identification with the unit is illustrated by the craftsman who, on being assigned to a unit, asked whether he should continue to wear his brown craftsman's overall, or change to a green one, as worn by the operators. He was advised to please himself. At first he kept to his brown overall, but within a month was seen to be wearing a green one.

Stanlow were also successful in reaching agreement with the craft unions (with one exception), that the sharing of work between crafts would not be based on a defined "shopping-list" of those specific items of work which could be shared, but rather on the broader principle that, within agreed limits, craftsmen could do anything for which they had available the time, tools and ability. The virtue of this more flexible arrangement was that it avoided a situation where relevant work might be refused by a craftsman on the grounds that it was not specifically itemised on the "shopping-list."

Provision was made for any training necessary to equip craftsmen to carry out work of a different craft, and a special joint committee of management representatives and shop stewards was set up, to ensure that the development of new working practices was in line with the principles and the spirit of work sharing, as agreed during the negotiations.

A three-month transition period was allowed in the agreement before the new working practices became operational. This gave time for training to take place and new administrative procedures to be set up. No major problems arose during this lead-in period, and this was due in part perhaps to a document circulated by the union officials, which urged craftsmen to have faith in the new deal and to co-operate in making it work. It was also due, no doubt, to the tremendous efforts taken by Stanlow to keep their managers and supervisors fully in the picture during the discussions and negotiations which had produced the new agreement.

Shell Haven

The negotiation of a new agreement with the TGWU at Shell Haven was a story of long and intensive collaboration between shop stewards and management representatives. The review which follows of the steps which led to final agreement with the union should be read in the context of the poor level of morale, and the long-standing history of industrial relations problems with which the refinery had had to contend over previous years.

The management was determined to extend the success gained in the operator JWP, and the East Site experiment, into a comprehensive productivity bargain, and were willing to invest a great deal of time and effort to this end. The concluding of a satisfactory bargain was seen as the primary way of putting the ideas of the philosophy statement into practice at shop floor level. It was an exercise in participation on the grand scale.

After the winding up of the JWP, the union asked the management to draft an agreement which would take into account the propositions debated by the JWP, and could serve as the basis for formal negotiation. The draft was produced, and contained as an essential feature the application to all the operating departments of the block team concept which had proved itself a success during the East Site experiment.

During the drafting period, and the early stages of negotiation, a steering committee made up of all department managers employing TGWU members, and personnel representatives, met periodically under the chairmanship of the manufacturing manager. In this way the line managers concerned were kept in the picture and were able to contribute to the development of the new agreement.

A copy of the draft agreement was given to all the TGWU shop stewards, who ensured that every employee who would be affected by it could see it. As a result, some ninety specific comments on the draft were fed back by the stewards to the negotiating team.

Also at this stage of the proceedings, each operating department manager presented his proposals on how the block team concept would be applied within his department to a meeting of his own men and the two senior shop stewards who sat on the negotiating team. Some useful ideas and suggestions for improvement emerged from these meetings.

When the draft was finalised, and the union had decided to recommend its acceptance to the membership, a secret ballot was organised by the union to be conducted at its branch offices. Before the ballot took place, however, an intensive briefing programme was carried out. Each department involved held meetings at which each shift of employees in turn were led through a detailed examination of the final proposals on which they would be voting. Each meeting normally lasted for four hours. They were run jointly by the department manager and his senior shop steward, and were attended also by one management representative and one senior shop steward from the negotiating team.

The secret ballot attracted a high poll of 80 per cent of the membership. The result was a rather narrow majority in favour of accepting the new agreement.

When the agreement had been cleared through the Department of Employment, the next phase was a lead-in period of four months to allow for training, and preparation for the radical changes involved.

Finally, drawing again on the experience of the East Site experiment, an implementation team was set up with the task of ensuring that the new agreement was fully and uniformly implemented and of dealing with any procedural problems that might arise. The team was made up of the two senior shop stewards who had been involved in the whole development of the agreement since the start of the JWP, a personnel man from the negotiating team and a line manager. They had to act unanimously as a team or refer problems to the management and the union for resolution.

The productivity agreement with the TGWU was clearly, therefore, costly in terms of the time and resources invested in it. Considering, however, the previous history of Shell Haven, and the unfavourable climate of pre-philosophy days, the outcome must rank as a very great success, and a tribute to the determination of both management and union representatives to make it so. It must also be seen as a striking example of the impact which the company philosophy programme had on some people's attitudes and motivation.

The bargain with the craft unions was not effective until November 1970. It was perhaps significant that before serious negotiation started the senior shop stewards who had been opposed to the whole notion of the philosophy process, and to the JWP, had moved out of their shop steward roles.

An interesting feature of the bargain was the final disappearance of an old Shell Haven custom which the management had been trying unsuccessfully to change for the previous ten years or more. The custom concerned the way in which work was carried out—and paid for—on major plant shutdowns. During such shutdowns, it is normal for certain maintenance tasks to be worked on continuously throughout the twenty-four hours each day, and for some craftsmen therefore to be assigned to work the night hours. Whilst logic directed that these men should be temporarily assigned to shift work for the period involved, the craftsmen refused to give up the traditional and lucrative custom of being treated as day workers, so that the whole of their working spell at night attracted overtime rates of payment.

In the November 1970 agreement, however, it was accepted that, in the context of the elimination of overtime payments, and the extension of job and time flexibility, such work on shutdowns should in future be covered by a system of temporary shift-work.

CONCLUSION

It seems clear that the productivity bargaining side of the company development programme has proved very successful. It is also clear that the refineries linked the development of the bargains very closely to the overall philosophy process. To what extent the success achieved in the bargaining depended on the effects of the philosophy dissemination programme it is not possible to measure exactly. Certainly it was the opinion of the managements concerned that the one could not have been achieved without the other.

Part Six
CONCLUSIONS

Chapter 16

Assessment of Results of the Company Development Programme

Towards the end of 1966, about one year after the development programme had been launched, the managing director asked for a review of what the programme had cost so far and what evidence there was of returns on the investment, however these might be measured.

It was recognised, of course, that this would be a first assessment of a long-term process which was still in its initial stages. The task of disseminating the philosophy statement was largely complete at Stanlow and Ardrossan, but was due to continue for some time at Shell Haven. The pilot projects at Stanlow were completing their first analytical phases but had not yet produced any action plans. The joint working parties were making some progress but had not yet reached the stage of putting forward recommendations for productivity bargaining.

It was also recognised that any attempt at assessment of results presented great difficulties of quantification even of the simplest kind. This applied to some of the investment costs, such as the expenditure of time by managers and others on the programme. It applied especially to the evaluation of many of the results achieved, owing to the position of the company in the Group and the lack of real economic yardsticks.

A further problem was to identify those changes or results which could be directly attributed to the effect of the philosophy programme. Some might have taken place without it, some might simply have been helped along by it.

Nevertheless, in spite of the difficulties, the need to attempt an assessment of progress was fully accepted by everyone.

171

METHOD OF ASSESSMENT

Devising a suitable method of carrying out the assessment was itself not a simple matter. Something was needed which would produce results for the managing director in a reasonably short space of time. It could not, therefore, be too complex, nor too time-consuming for the people who would be involved.

With the help of the refineries, Tavistock and ERP designed a brief questionnaire for completion by all the department managers in the company, since they were seen as the key people who would initiate change. The design of the questionnaire was based on the idea that it would seek to measure the amount of movement which had taken place in the directions indicated as desirable by the statement of objectives and philosophy.

Department managers were asked to report any changes which had occurred in their departments since January 1966

1   Changes in organisation or procedures, in the following areas:
(a) Redefinition of job responsibilities
(b) Improved communications
(c) Redefinition of objectives
(d) Review of policies or procedural rules
(e) Awareness or application of joint optimisation
(f) Additional training at all levels

2   Changes in job design so as better to meet psychological requirements:
(a) Variety of tasks
(b) Job targets and knowledge of results
(c) Learning on the job
(d) Increased areas for decision taking
(e) Increased participation in problem solving
(f) Support and recognition
(g) Relation of job to company or community
(h) Desirable future

3   Signs of increased responsibility and commitment, or of changed attitudes

4   Evidence of improved performance in meeting the specific objectives in section 2 of the philosophy statement:
(a) Meeting current or emerging requirements more effectively
(b) Securing better information to do job, or getting job redefined
(c) Personal growth
(d) Safety
(e) Pollution

FIGURE 16:1   QUESTIONNAIRE FOR DEPARTMENT MANAGERS
Used in 1967 assessment development programme

In this context, the philosophy statement indicated that the company should be seeking:

1   *Changes in organisation or procedures,* which would make possible:
2   *Redesigning of jobs at all levels,* leading to:
3   *Increased personal commitment and responsibility,* making possible:
4   *More effective pursuit of company objectives.*

The questionnaire accordingly asked for any relevant changes to be logged in all four areas, it being recognised that the first two areas would represent investment in the change process, whereas the latter two would indicate evidence of a return on investment. At this early stage in the programme, it was anticipated that most changes would have occurred in the first two areas, and fewer in the latter two, pay-off, areas.

The detailed questions posed are shown in Figure 16:1. Each refinery added to its own questionnaire sheets an actual example of change against each question, to help department managers understand what was required. They were asked to report all relevant changes, irrespective of whether they were, in their opinion, wholly, partly, or not at all attributable to the effect of the philosophy process. It was considered that the volume and nature of the changes reported, when compared with the normal tempo of change in previous years, would of themselves give a gross indication of the extent of cause and effect involved.

In addition to the questionnaire data, refineries were also asked to:

1   Summarise the direct and indirect costs they had incurred, such as conference charges and managers' time
2   Report on general operational performance levels since the programme was launched
3   Produce data to indicate the general level of morale: for example, sickness and absence statistics, labour turnover records and safety records

RESULTS OF ASSESSMENT

The results of the refinery assessment exercises were presented to the managing director in April 1967. He spent a day at Shell Haven and at Stanlow reviewing the outcome with the management teams, both general managers being present at both events. The overall picture which emerged from this first attempt at evaluation is summarised below.

Costs

The direct costs of the company development programme up to January 1967 totalled approximately £55 000, for all the locations and head office. This was made up mainly of the cost of running some seventy residential dissemination conferences and the fees paid to Tavistock.

Indirect costs were not quantified but showed that managers at senior levels had spent on average some 3 to 4 per cent of their normal working hours on planning and carrying out the dissemination programme. An enormous effort had also been put in outside normal working hours, particularly by the top managers.

Achievements

The data provided by the department managers via the questionnaires showed that there had been a very large number of changes in the desired direction and that the tempo of change far exceeded that of previous years. Few of the changes had been objectively quantified and there was a wide variation in the importance and significance of individual items, but taken together they represented a clear and positive movement towards the objectives embodied in the philosophy statement.

A greater volume of changes was reported at Stanlow than at Shell Haven, which was consistent with the faster rate of dissemination adopted by Stanlow management. There were also differences between departments within refineries, the operating departments tending to report more changes than any others.

The profile of changes as distributed between the four areas designated in the questionnaire followed the anticipated pattern: that is, more changes were reported in the first two investment areas, and fewer in the latter two pay-off areas. Inconsistencies and ambiguities in departmental reporting, however, did not permit an overall presentation in a reliable quantitative form, despite efforts to achieve one. This was disappointing but understandable in the circumstances, since the exercise had been carried out with some urgency, and for operational rather than research purposes. Nevertheless, the returns of the twenty-three service and auxiliary departments at Stanlow were made in a more consistent manner, with the aid of the personnel department, and could be tabulated with some confidence. The pattern of changes which they reported was as follows:

	AREA OF CHANGE	NUMBER OF DEPARTMENTS REPORTING CHANGE
1	Organisational or procedural	15
2	Job design	10
3	Responsibility and commitment	10
4	Improved performance	5

Most of the changes reported in area 3 were a fall-out from the dissemination conferences, rather than the result of changes in job design.

The profile for the operating departments at Stanlow was similar to that for the service departments. Their progress was, however, better, since they registered considerably more changes under each heading, although the ambiguities made detailed analysis impossible.

All locations reported some favourable results in common. These were:

1 Contrary to what might have been expected at the start of such an intensive development programme, there had been no adverse effect on refinery operations during 1966. This meant that the considerable extra work involved had been absorbed by extra effort on the part of the people concerned.

2 The healthy state of morale in the company implied by point 1 above was confirmed by such morale indicators as existed. Although the time span of one year was too short to draw any significant conclusions, in no case was any adverse movement noted in sickness, absence or accident rates, or in labour turnover. An interesting contrast which emerged was that whereas absence of hourly paid employees due to sickness decreased marginally at Stanlow during 1966, it increased markedly at the adjoining research centre. The only apparent explanation for this difference was that Stanlow staff were participating in the philosophy programme whereas the research centre staff were not.

3 The dissemination conferences had of themselves produced several valuable fall-outs. For example, they had clearly developed the skills of many of the senior people involved in leading them; they had opened up new channels of communication within and between departments; and they had created a climate in which people at many levels felt free to ask questions in areas previously shrouded in secrecy, or to demand better information as an aid to improved performance.

4 The joint working parties were ensuring the discussion of important

issues throughout the refineries, and were responsible for considerable personal development in some of their members.

5   There had been evidence of significant changes in attitude in people at various levels, including many on the shop floor. Some of these changes had led to demonstrable improvements in productivity.

6   There had been a focusing of attention on the need for more effective manpower planning and on the need for better training and development of people at all levels.

7   There had been, in general, a very favourable response to the programme from the trade unions.

Specific examples
In order to give an idea of the sort of specific changes reported by the department managers, some typical examples are summarised below, under each of the four main areas of the questionnaire.

1   *Organisational and procedural*
   (*a*) Discussion and agreement of objectives at departmental meetings. This was reported to have been done, in whole or in part, by the majority of managers at Stanlow
   (*b*) Elimination, on an experimental basis, of clocking arrangements for hourly paid employees, by most departments at Stanlow
   (*c*) Establishment of a special studies department at Shell Haven (headed by the resource manager) to conduct a five-year resources survey as a basis for matching manpower to the forward technical programme
   (*d*) Setting up of additional training programmes for process operators in several Stanlow departments
2   *Job design*
   (*a*) Increased authority for materials buyers to purchase items, at Stanlow and Shell Haven
   (*b*) Extension of area of responsibility for operators on wax unit at Stanlow, who were given discretion to use a new instrument on the unit (the gas liquid chromatograph)
   (*c*) Enlargement of jobs of laboratory supervisors at Shell Haven through delegation of much wider responsibilities
   (*d*) Involvement of operators in the design of instrumentation for the new boilers at Stanlow
3   *Responsibility and commitment*
   (*a*) Improved attitudes reported in craftsmen and installation operators at Ardrossan

(b) Relaxation of all demarcation restrictions volunteered by craftsmen at Stanlow during the major rehabilitation of the distillation unit after a fire

(c) Acceptance by operators at Shell Haven of the need for a sophisticated in-line blending system which would require fewer people to operate it, leading to their involvement in its layout and to its smooth introduction

(d) Co-operation of craftsmen at Stanlow working without supervision in an isolated pumphouse

4   *Improved performance*

(a) Increased productivity with reduced crew and 50 per cent less overtime reported by bitumen department at Stanlow

(b) Greatly improved rail car filling at Stanlow with the same number of people

(c) Improved performance in meeting rushed orders for expikote exports without additional manpower at Stanlow

(d) Improved reporting of results in Shell Haven laboratory as a result of increased responsibility and initiative

(e) Much increased level of production in Stanlow engineering workshops, with only marginal increase in man-hours

Problems

Whilst the overall impression created by the results of the assessment review was, therefore, very positive, a few negative points also emerged. These were:

1   There was still insufficient understanding at various levels of the concept of joint optimisation and some people accordingly did not see how to introduce change in their own areas.

2   Some people at the supervisory level were tending to see the development programme as aimed solely at improving conditions for the hourly paid employees.

3   There were some fears that the process of involving people in making decisions which would directly affect their own jobs was time-consuming and might lead to a situation of management by committee.

4   The uneven level of progress and development at the different locations was tending to lead to interlocation competitiveness of a negative kind, which was hindering the spread of experience and learning.

These problems indicated a need to reinforce understanding of the key concepts of the philosophy and to provide help to department managers wishing to bring about change. They were a contributory factor leading to the development of the two analytical methods described in Chapter 12. They also led to the setting up of a special team to study the role of the supervisor in the refineries. It was expected that the process of departmental meetings which had now begun would serve to correct the misapprehensions about the philosophy programme's aim and implications.

POSITIVE DEVELOPMENTS SINCE THE 1967 ASSESSMENT

Some of the major developments and achievements since the assessment review in 1967 have already been described in preceding chapters: the outcome of the pilot projects at Stanlow, leading to the development and application of the two analytical methods; the contribution of the joint working parties to the successful negotiation of productivity bargains at all three refineries; and the establishment at Teesport of an organisation with an unusually high level of joint optimisation.

The task of preparing for and negotiating the productivity bargains assumed very great importance, particularly at Shell Haven, from 1967 until they were all finally completed in 1970. This was logical because it was seen as vital to secure really effective agreements with the trade unions. It was also highly successful, since it transformed the industrial relations climate at Shell Haven and permitted plans for plant expansions to proceed there. It did, however, tend to absorb the greater part of the implementation effort during that period.

In spite of the concentration of resources on productivity bargaining, a number of additional implementation measures were developed. By 1967, the philosophy programme had created a climate across the company which favoured and supported efforts to put its concepts into practice. A philosophy statement was seen as providing a framework of values within which a variety of experiments could be tried out.

An opportunity to test out these values, and the whole concept of the development programme, in the wider Shell world, was provided when the leader of the ERP team was invited to talk about it to the members of a number of study group programmes run in London by Group training division for senior managers from the Group's worldwide organisation. These events took place during 1966 and 1967, when the way the project would develop was still uncertain. The material was presented in the form of a live case study. The members, representing many nationalities and coming from many different environments, were asked to study the material in syndicates and then to comment on the validity of the approach adopted by Shell UK Limited. They were also asked to consider what future developments should be aimed at and to make recommendations and predictions. At the final session, the managing director of Shell UK Limited joined the study group to hear the syndicates report back their views and to comment on their proposals. The outcome of these events was a strong and, in some cases, enthusiastic endorsement of what Shell UK Limited was setting out to do.

Some of the ways in which implementation measures were tried out in the company are summarised below.

Staff appraisal

A need which was recognised early in the development programme was to institutionalise the philosophy within the company: in other words, to create policies and procedures which would reflect its values. This had been done effectively at Teesport but was more difficult to achieve in the older refineries.

An important example of an area where change of this nature was seen as necessary was the staff appraisal system. If managers were to be encouraged to devote their energies to managing a socio-technical system, and to protecting and developing their resources, it was vital that they should not continue to be assessed mainly on their handling of the technical system alone. The need expressed by people at early dissemination conferences for assurances that the development programme was supported by top management, was an indication that they did not want to embark on new ways of managing, if the people at the top were going to use old criteria for judging their performance. A complicating factor was that staff appraisal of senior and middle managers was based on a system recommended by Group personnel division.

In 1969, Group personnel division adopted an amended form of appraisal based on assessing a man's performance according to the extent to which he had achieved specific work targets previously agreed with his manager. Each year, therefore, new targets would be agreed, against which performance would be reviewed and assessed in twelve months' time.

This change was welcomed in the company, since it was consistent with the concepts of the philosophy and it also served to reinforce the

N

attention already paid at the refineries to redefinition of objectives at department, unit and individual levels.

ERP, however, considered that the system could be further improved. In collaboration with Stanlow, they developed an additional assessment form, designed specifically to judge a manager's ability to manage the social system. This form is currently being used on an experimental basis, in addition to the formal appraisal sheet, for the assessment of supervisory staff at Stanlow.

The form suggests that a man's performance *vis-à-vis* management of the social system should be reviewed under four headings. Examples of the factors included in each area are given below:

1   *Maintenance of human resources*
     (a) Knowledge of work problems of individuals under his control
     (b) Extent to which skills of individuals are kept up to date
     (c) Competence in handling conflict (for example, industrial relations problems)
2   *Development of human resources*
     (a) Ability of deputy to assume control in his absence
     (b) Extent of training carried out for individuals under his control
     (c) Extent to which opportunities are created for the exercise of the developed skills back on the job.
3   *Motivation of human resources*
     (a) Extent of successful delegation
     (b) Adequacy in building a group of individuals into a team
     (c) Extent to which the group under his control is kept informed of its strengths and weaknesses
4   *General characteristics of managerial role*
     (a) Extent of real innovation in relation to the social system
     (b) Communication ability: written, spoken (individual), spoken (to group)
     (c) Interpersonal competence, in relation to subordinates, boss, others

It is anticipated that this experimental approach will be modified and improved, but it is considered that an assessment on these lines, taken in conjunction with the normal appraisal of his technical abilities, will allow a more relevant judgement of a man's performance and potential as a manager. It will also highlight those areas in which he needs extra personal development and where appropriate objectives can be formulated each year for him to work towards in parallel with his operational targets.

Management by objectives
The effort to establish a hierarchy of objectives in the refineries, deriving from the company's operational and social objectives, was a continuing one. In late 1969, the Shell Haven management decided to introduce a formal system of management by objectives to reinforce this process on the refinery. It was significant that the internal direction of this effort was put in the hands of the special studies department, with the intention of ensuring that the system was applied in a way which was consistent with the values of the philosophy and not, as can sometimes happen, as a means of enforcing more autocratic control over people's performance.

Trade union agreements
Whilst the content of the company's agreements with the trade unions was significantly changed and improved as the result of the productivity bargains, the head office personnel department was concerned thereafter to bring the procedural clauses governing such matters as disciplinary action and the resolution of conflict more into line with the general aims of the philosophy.

In consultation with the refineries, and before approaching the trade unions, they are currently considering how the clauses might be so designed that they would induce the maximum sense of joint responsibility between company and unions for seeing that they were adhered to, reduce the area of conflict and facilitate change through some form of joint problem-solving mechanisms.

Communications
The philosophy programme has brought about lasting improvements in communications at Shell Haven and Stanlow. Most departments now hold regular meetings, monthly or more frequently, with representatives from all levels of employees. At Shell Haven, for example, it has been found that these regular departmental meetings handle much of the business which used previously to be referred as problems to the central shop stewards committees. This has resulted in an up-grading of the level of discussion and a more positive role for the shop stewards committees. At Stanlow, the work of the central works council has progressively been decentralised in a similar way, so that most problems are now solved within the system of departmental meetings.

Induction and training
New employees at various levels, including graduates, operators and apprentices, who join the refineries, are currently given the background history of the company development programme and taken through the main points of the philosophy document, in differing degrees of detail. Refinery training programmes are not based directly on the document, but the link between their content and the objective of encouraging and enabling people to develop and realise their potentialities is usually made clear.

Participation
The involvement of people on the shop floor in the planning and design of projects which would previously have been completed without any reference to them is a continuing process. At Shell Haven, for example, the implementation team, set up in 1969 to help smooth the introduction of the new TGWU productivity agreement, was asked to deal also with the problem of integrating into the agreement the employees of the adjoining installation site (London and Thames Haven Oil Wharves), which had just been purchased by Shell. This presented a very complicated problem but the team, made up of a line manager, two senior shop stewards and a personnel man, tackled it in a joint problem-solving way and produced very successful results.

More recently, representatives of craftsmen and operators have been invited to join supervisors and managers on a committee to participate in the design and setting up of a new process unit at Shell Haven.

Job enrichment
In seeking to explore alternative methods of redesigning jobs, Stanlow carried out some projects during 1969 using the Herzberg approach to job enrichment (described in Chapter 1). With the help of an outside consultant, Bill Paul, and one of their own personnel men, they focussed on enriching the jobs of supervisors in three of the operating departments.

There were two main differences between Stanlow's use of the approach and Herzberg's original method. First, no control group was established, because each operating department is different from the others. Second, rather than having specific changes decided upon at two levels about the supervisors concerned, the supervisors themselves were involved in discussing the proposals for changing their jobs and in deciding what could be implemented. This approach was felt to be more productive and certainly more in line with the company philosophy.

Whilst the changes implemented in the three departments differed, the general aim was to enrich the supervisor's role through giving him:

1   Greater responsibility for training and assessment of his men
2   Increased financial responsibility and authority
3   Greater authority in selecting his men
4   Increased personal development through special project work and training
5   Increased responsibility for formal disciplinary action
6   Increased authority for dealing with suggestions under the suggestion scheme

The three department managers were favourably impressed with the outcome of the projects. It was the general view, however, that these types of changes could not be introduced on a blanket basis across the refinery. A specific programme for change would need to be tailored to each department's particular circumstances and needs.

Role of supervisor

A special study carried out in 1969 was concerned with the role and task of supervision in the company. Taking the philosophy concepts as a basis, the study examined what general changes would need to be made to help supervisors meet their psychological needs more effectively. The supervisor's responsibility for controlling a social system was recognised, as was his need to be able to identify himself clearly as a vital part of the company's management.

The study resulted in a re-evaluation of the supervisors' position in the salary structure and a general recommendation that their area of discretion should be widened and their level of responsibility increased. Detailed implementation of these recommendations was left to each location and the experience gained at Stanlow through their job enrichment projects was seen as useful and relevant.

SOME NEGATIVE ASPECTS

There have also been some negative aspects of this history of the development programme since the formal assessment in early 1967. The salient ones are described below.

Top level support

There was a lack, after mid-1967, of continuing visible commitment at the top to the philosophy programme. When Shell UK Limited assumed its present form in mid-1967, it was headed by a new chief executive who was responsible not only for the previous company's refining activities but also, among other things, for Shell's rapidly growing exploration and production activities in the North Sea. These organisational changes provoked renewed requests from the refineries for assurances that the top management of the enlarged company endorsed and supported the philosophy programme. Tavistock and ERP drafted an amended philosophy statement, which was based on the same key concepts, but tailored to the company's enlarged role. It was hoped that this document would be discussed and accepted by the new management team, thus clearly and formally endorsing the continued development of the philosophy programme.

Unfortunately, the structural reorganisation preceded by only a few months the 1967 oil crisis caused by the war in the Middle East and the closure of the Suez Canal. Soon afterwards the Nigerian civil war caused a further disruption of crude oil supplies. The result of these crises was an extended period of intensive activity for all those concerned, particularly in head office, in coping with the problems of the supply situation. No opportunity therefore arose for consideration of the new draft document.

The effect of this situation was that, although the refineries were assured that there was no question of the company development programme ceasing to be supported at the top, this was, from the refineries' point of view, less obvious and less certain than before. This tended to have an inhibiting effect on people's willingness to embark on change.

Transfers and retirements

During the years 1967–8, which were highly important for the implementation phase of the programme, a considerable number of changes in job assignments took place. This had the effect of reducing drastically the level of skilled and experienced resources available to help the process develop. Some of these changes were unavoidable, such as the retirement of the managing director and of the general manager at Stanlow. Others were the result of career planning moves for the individuals concerned, which caused big changes in the ERP team.

The effect of these internal changes was aggravated by the departure during the same period of the two principal Tavistock participants in the programme, Eric Trist to the United States, and Fred Emery, first to the US and then to Australia. In mid-1968, of the joint Tavistock and ERP teams who had most closely been involved in the drafting of the philosophy statement and the planning of the 1965 Selsdon Park Conference, only one person remained. Of the eleven senior managers who had participated in the conference, six remained.

Whilst any change process such as the company development programme must clearly be strong enough to support some pruning of its skilled resource people, the severity of the 1967–8 dispersal of resources, combined with the necessary focus of effort at the refineries on the productivity deals and the head office preoccupation with supply problems, undoubtedly hindered a fuller realisation of the potential implementation developments at that time.

Lack of regular assessment of progress
At the conclusion of the formal assessment of progress in 1967, it was agreed in principle by the company's management team that there should be further regular assessments at intervals of not more than twelve months. This was considered important, not only to keep track of the level of success being achieved, and to identify problem areas, but also to demonstrate to everyone in the company that the success of the development programme was of vital and continuing concern to the top management of the company.

Preparations were accordingly made for an assessment survey in 1968. Whereas the original review had concentrated on the views of the department managers, this one was intended to seek the opinions of all levels of employees in the company and to produce, therefore, a more comprehensive picture of the progress being made. A questionnaire was designed with the idea that it could be repeated at intervals, and arrangements were made to secure data in a more reliably quantifiable form, so as to provide a trend line based on comparable information. In the event, the 1968 assessment did not take place, owing partly to the severe pressure of external events and, partly, to the reduced level of the ERP team, who would have been responsible for the administration and co-ordination of the survey.

CONCLUSIONS

The evidence presented earlier in this chapter demonstrates clearly that the philosophy programme has produced some very dramatic successes.

There are many indications that the process is continuing and that further improvements are likely to follow.

The negative aspects of the programme so far have also been noted: for example, the dispersal of the original leaders and resource people, the introduction of new leaders who were not party to the launching of the programme and who have left many people in the company unconvinced that they are committed to its ideas and the lack, since 1967, of any formal attempt to assess the progress being made. There is no doubt that these factors, combined with the pressure of external events and the natural tendency of people to revert, in a climate of uncertainty, to previously established procedures when confronted with problems, have led to a loss of momentum in the development programme since 1968, to some regression (as at Teesport) towards the old way of doing things, and indeed, to the future of the programme being put in question —despite its achievements—in some parts of the organisation.

Whether, therefore, the values and concepts of the philosophy statement are now sufficiently well embodied in the organisation to withstand any future set-backs, it is still too early to judge. The indications are that they are, but the next five years will show.

In the final chapter, an attempt is made to explore the wider implications of the development programme.

Chapter 17

Implications for Managers and Unions

This book has described the attempt of an oil manufacturing company in the UK industrial environment to bring about changes that would make possible a higher level of motivation and commitment to company objectives on the part of all its employees, leading to an enhanced level of performance.

The purpose of this final chapter is to consider what wider implications can be drawn for managers and trade unions from this particular experience. In order to arrive at these, it will be useful to review briefly what were the distinctive characteristics of Shell UK Limited's company development programme.

DISTINCTIVE CHARACTERISTICS OF
DEVELOPMENT PROGRAMME

1 A small team was set up to study the company's long-standing motivation problem on a full-time basis and to propose long-term plans for attempting to solve it.

2 A close collaborative working relationship was established between outside social science resources from the Tavistock Institute and internal resource people in the company. One result was a very considerable transfer of knowledge and skills into the organisation.

3 A document was produced stating explicitly the objectives the company would work towards and the management philosophy, or values, which would be used to guide decision making in pursuing them. A

key feature of the document was a reconciliation of the company's economic and social objectives.

4   The top management team of the company, led by the managing director, was committed to the objectives and philosophy, and to seeking commitment to them throughout the organisation. The management team met at critical decision-points in the programme, to decide on and guide the general course it should take.

5   In order to secure this wider commitment a complex dissemination programme was developed. Through a cascade of conferences at each location, large numbers of employees at all levels were able to test out the objectives and philosophy for themselves. The remaining employees had an opportunity to do this through departmental meetings, so that eventually all the employees in the company were included.

6   The dissemination process was dynamic, not stereotyped. This led to different method being tried out and to each location's developing programmes which were best suited to its own refinery situation.

7   The dissemination process achieved considerable success in securing a widespread understanding of, and commitment to, the company's objectives and philosophy. It also produced a minority of highly enthusiastic employees who represented the critical mass who led the process of implementation.

8   Trade union representatives, both outside officials and internal shop stewards, reacted with only few exceptions very favourably to the company's intentions and offered their support.

9   The dissemination programme developed new skills in many people and created a climate in the company which permitted and encouraged the trying out of new ideas. Many new things were tried and, although they did not all fully achieve their purpose, they contributed to the overall learning and development and provided a stepping stone to the next move forward.

10   An important example of this type of innovation was the setting up of the joint working parties, whose new role and new frame of reference were accepted by the majority of the shop stewards and by all the trade union officials. Although they did not fully complete their tasks, the work they did made a valuable contribution to the productivity bargains which followed. The East Site experiment at Shell Haven was in itself a remarkable achievement and it sprang from the suggestion of the TGWU senior shop stewards.

11   The outcome of the productivity bargaining, after the expenditure of much time and effort, was also very successful. More important

than the content of the bargains—significant as that also was—was the manner in which they were arrived at. Both management representatives and union representatives were dedicated to the bargaining's success and shared to a greater extent than ever before the same frame of reference. The level of participation on the part of shop stewards in the formulation of the bargains and the level of effective communication with the shop-floor employees was exceptionally high. The result was commitment to the content and spirit of the deals, not merely a collection of unenforceable agreements.

12 A more general result of the new climate and the new collaborative working relationships between shop stewards and management has been a vast improvement in the industrial relations situation at Shell Haven. General morale has improved accordingly.

13 The other major field where innovation took place was in the design of jobs. Here again, partial success in one venture did not stop progress, but led to the start of another. The process was again dynamic.

14 The pilot projects at Stanlow created great opportunities for learning and indicated good possibilities for improvement in performance levels. Although their full potential for producing change was not realised, and frustration was caused by the long timescale involved, they achieved some success and also led to another important development.

15 The development of the two simplified methods of analysing existing systems was again a great learning experience in which many people in the company were involved. The application of the methods at Stanlow showed good and promising results. As with the earlier pilot projects, they demonstrated how shop-floor employees could contribute significantly to these results. The nine-step method of socio-technical analysis has also been found valuable, both as a training tool and in its practical application in places outside the company.

16 The largest-scale application of the philosophy concepts in the company was in the design of the social system at Teesport. The principle of joint optimisation was consciously and carefully applied, with highly successful results.

17 There was a wide variety of other implementation measures all undertaken within the framework of the philosophy concepts. They included changes in the staff appraisal system and in manpower planning, job enrichment projects, and so on.

18 The development programme has been subjected to many counter-

vailing pressures. Some have been internal, such as the retirement or transfer of key people, both in management and among the resource people. Others have been external, such as the disruption of crude supplies by war, or the pressures felt at Teesport to regress to old norms.

19   The evaluation of progress in early 1967 was a valuable exercise. It gave evidence of the great impact the development programme was having on the company, it indicated problems which needed attention and it demonstrated the continuing and serious commitment to the programme of the company's top management. The lack of any further formal evaluation has been a weakness in the programme.

IMPLICATIONS

The following would seem to be the main implications which can be drawn from the experience gained so far of the company development programme:

1   The problem of alienation of people at work, even when long standing, is not insoluble. Provided the effort by management is serious, well-directed and determined, it is possible to improve the climate of a whole organisation and to create conditions in which people at all levels, including shop-floor employees, will become committed to organisation objectives and motivated to do their jobs efficiently.

2   The knowledge, skills and experience of social scientists can make a very great contribution to undertakings of this kind. If outside people are assisting the organisation, there should be a commitment to develop inside the organisation the necessary skills and knowledge to help carry the programme forward and eventually to take over most of the work.

3   The need in an organisation contemplating such change for the top management to be committed to the change programme is absolute.

4   The objectives and philosophy of an organisation—whether written down or not—govern the way it runs its affairs and determine the way employees feel about the organisation and about their jobs. They are of real concern and importance to employees at all levels, including the shop floor.

5   If the objectives and philosophy of an organisation are consistent with the needs, aspirations and values of the employees, their open adoption by the top management and managers down the line will

induce commitment to them by most employees, if they are given the opportunity to explore their implications.

6   The concepts developed by Tavistock, and embodied in the Shell UK Limited philosophy statement, are such that most people in an organisation will recognise their validity and appropriateness. Moreover, the application of the principle of joint optimisation of the socio-technical system offers a way of improving job design to the benefit of both the employee, through greater satisfaction in his work, and the organisation, through an improved level of performance.

7   Provided the union representatives involved, both external and internal, perceive the management as sincere in its intentions, they are likely to support a change undertaking of this kind. Freed from much unnecessary conflict caused by opposed objectives, they are likely to adopt a new role and to bring their great experience and knowledge of the work to bear on the problems of job redesign. They are capable of significant innovation.

8   A dynamic approach to a change undertaking, whilst more risky than a stereotyped or routinised approach, offers the opportunity of developments over a much wider field and much better adapted to the needs of the situation.

9   If productivity bargains are part of the change programme, the most important thing is the manner in which they are achieved. In order to get the people who will be affected by it committed to the content of a bargain, it is necessary to explore new channels of communication and develop new ways of participation so that, as far as possible, the content can be jointly developed by the two parties. Commitment to a lesser bargain, which will be operated, is better than non-commitment to a greater bargain, which will not.

10   A change undertaking of this nature is a long-term business and requires a large-scale effort. The employment of resource people, whose task is to help the management make the programme a success, should be planned and maintained accordingly. Countervailing pressures will inevitably arise and the management and resource people must be robust enough to withstand them over the long term. Special arrangements might be needed to keep managers and internal resource people on the task for a longer period than would be normal and to reward them accordingly.

11   There is a need to ensure that people's expectations of change are pitched at a reasonable level. They should not expect overdramatic changes, nor expect things to happen too quickly. In a large-scale

change programme, some set-backs and disappointments are inevitable and should be accepted as part of the pattern of growth.

12   Plans should be made from the start for some form of evaluation of the change process. Top management should commit itself to assess regularly the progress that is being made and the problems that are arising, thus demonstrating to the whole organisation its continuing involvement in the undertaking.

EPILOGUE

Epilogue and Summary

From the Tavistock Perspective

by ERIC TRIST

One morning in May 1965 the author of this book, Paul Hill, came along from Shell Refining (as the company was then called) together with Harman Bell, a colleague from Shell International, to the Tavistock Institute of Human Relations to discuss with Fred Emery and myself some research that we might possibly undertake with them. They explained that at a recent top management conference a company development programme, proposed after extensive preparation by the staff resource group headed by Hill, had been accepted and that one of the main proposals involved the working out of a new management philosophy.

This philosophy would have to fulfil two related purposes: to be a guide to managerial decision making during a period of increasing technological change; to be a stabiliser during a period of increasing industrial unrest. It would, therefore, have to be seen as relevant to the operations of the company as a manufacturing concern—and in this sense to be "valid." Equally it would have to be acceptable not only to all levels of management but to the workers and their trade unions. This latter requirement related the philosophy proposal to the other main proposal in the company development programme. This was concerned with establishing the conditions under which genuine productivity bargaining could take place of a kind which would transform the relationship of the company with its hourly paid employees.

They then told us that it had been further agreed that the company should seek social science assistance in developing a relevant and acceptable statement of philosophy. We were not a little taken aback. No

O   195

company had ever brought such a problem to the Institute before. There were no ready-made answers in the literature. We would, indeed, have to put our thinking caps on if we were to make a contribution to such a problem.

We had, however, one clue from some of our recent theoretical work as to why a company such as Shell might be in search of a new philosophy to manage its refineries. This work was concerned with identifying possible lines of organisational response for enterprises confronted with the need to adapt to an accelerating rate of technological change under conditions of rising uncertainty and complexity (Emery & Trist, 1965). In this situation an organisation would only retain its cohesion and move in an appropriate direction if the majority of its members subscribed to a common set of values. These values would have to be relevant to the character of its tasks and to the emergent processes in its technology and environment. The explication of a self-consistent set of relevant values and the teasing out of their implications for all fields of the company's activities and for the needs of its employees at all levels would involve the formulation of a statement of philosophy.

The more familiar types of organisation which conform to the bureaucratic model which has been successful in industrial societies when the pace of change was slower and the degree of uncertainty and complexity were less, seem to be becoming more and more ill-suited to the challenges of the turbulent world which the last third of the twentieth century is bringing into existence. Their rigidities and tendencies to treat people as expendable commodities or replaceable machine parts is increasing alienation when commitment is more than ever becoming required. The class of organisations most exposed to the ensuing problems and likely to be most concerned therefore to do something about them are companies in the large-scale science-based industries. Shell Refining, a member of the Royal Dutch/Shell Group, was just such a company.

There was a strong likelihood, it seemed to us, that a number of its key members had, through their own experience and in their own terms, reached conclusions similar to our own—otherwise Paul Hill would never have put forward the type of programme he had proposed and this would never have been accepted by the managing director and his senior colleagues after thorough discussion in a new type of conference about a new type of issue.

To advance social science understanding in this area the Institute needed a company to work with which had very considerable capacity to confront the basic issues and thereafter to move decisively in the directions indicated. Any such company would need from social scientists a type of analysis and conceptualisation of the problems involved which, as well as being sound theoretically, could be made in a way which would speak directly both to its present condition and its view of its foreseeable future. The best way of achieving this would be for the social scientists to work in close conjunction with an appropriate internal staff resource group. This seemed to be available through Paul Hill. What was offered to management would then be co-produced. It would already have built into it a knowledge and understanding of the company not possible for outsiders to obtain.

The first task therefore was to find out whether Shell Refining and the Tavistock could accept each other in these complementary roles to the point of being willing jointly to commit themselves to what would inevitably be a prolonged, large-scale, costly and high-risk adventure in action research. Once embarked upon, it would be likely to extend to the limit the capacities—and patience—of those most closely involved. The only way to find out whether the company and the Institute should undertake any such joint venture was to try to see how far we could get with the initial task, which was to produce a draft philosophy statement and then to check this out with senior management.

The first research task therefore was a conceptual one. Any valid and acceptable philosophy for the two related purposes which had been indicated would have to postulate the existence of a social as well as an economic objective for the company. This meant reconciling the one with the other. Satisfactory criteria for doing this had never been established. A first step towards effecting the reconciliation was found by working out the implications of a basic duality: that the assets of the company were at the same time the resources of society. The assets it "owned," most especially its human assets, were not owned absolutely but conditionally. The conditions of the company's being allowed to continue to use them were that these resources would not be exploited or degraded but protected and developed. The next step was to consider how far the acceptance of such a social objective would be consistent with the economic objective—the goal of long-term profitability. Consistency was found to lie in the fact that the social objective, in committing the company not to waste resources, committed it thereby to seek long-term profitability exclusively by increasing productive efficiency. This ruled out market manipulation on the one hand and restrictive practices on the other, but raised the question of how best productive efficiency could be increased.

The answer to this question lay in the demonstration that productive efficiency could best be increased by the "joint optimisation of the technical and social systems," not by exclusive concentration on the technical side. The characteristics and capabilities of people are different from those of machines. In any system which requires both, the distinctive requirements of each have to be met. This means designing jobs and organisational structures so that human as well as technical needs can be met. In this way the human, as well as the material, resources used by the company would be protected and developed so that the social objective could be met in the context of the economic objective.

In short, the economic objective supplies the necessary condition but the social objective the sufficient condition for the survival and growth of the enterprise. The fundamental fallacy is to suppose that the necessary and sufficient conditions both lie in the economic objective; yet this has been the traditional assumption. The social objective is not simply a constraint on the economic objective; one is the co-producer of the other. A related fallacy is to suppose that the technology supplies both the necessary and sufficient conditions for productive efficiency, whereas this is a function of the joint optimisation of the human and technical factors which have different but complementary characteristics.

The special relevance of these ideas to the company lay in the fact that the core tasks of the workers in its process technology—and this also goes in large measure for the maintenance crafts—consist of "information handling." Information handling constitutes the basic nature of work in the technologies of what has come to be known as the Second Industrial Revolution. Rather than physical or manipulative skills, it requires perceptual and conceptual skills which involve anticipatory decision making requiring the exercise of a great deal of initiative and self-supervision. In such circumstances alienation is unacceptable, not merely undesirable. Commitment, therefore, becomes mandatory; but commitment cannot be forced, it can only be given. Authoritarianism is out.

A company with these requirements indeed needed to develop an operating philosophy which could be freely accepted by all its members. Such acceptance constituted a pre-condition for resolving long-standing and inhibiting conflicts between management and labour and for releasing creative potential at all levels. Without the transformation of climate that this would bring about the outlook was poor for building up the organisational capability adaptively to accept a faster change rate.

These ideas provided the foundations for a scenario worked out jointly by a sub-group of the Tavistock research team and of the internal resource group so that full account could be taken of the idiomatic features and circumstances of the company. This then served as a text on the basis of which top management could work through the full complexity of the issues involved until they had satisfied themselves that they had arrived at a statement of company objectives and philosophy to which they could commit themselves. This was accomplished in a residential conference in October 1965 which constituted the second critical top management event associated with the company development programme—the first having been the March conference which had sanctioned the launching of the programme. The conference was an intense experience, intellectually and emotionally, for all who participated. It brought the philosophy into existence.

Yet it would be of little avail if it existed simply in the minds of a handful of senior managers. To have any chance of being effective it would have to be disseminated throughout the entire organisation, and this comprised some 6000 people. Those who had attended the top management conference, however, were clear that this had to be done; and done moreover in some such way as they themselves had experienced. This would be a prodigious undertaking. Nevertheless, it was decided to do it. The design of the dissemination process, therefore, became the second research task.

Very little is known in social science about how to bring about relatively rapid value change in areas of central concern in large organisational populations. Usually such value changes come about very slowly —over a period of several years. Unless we learn how to bring them about much more rapidly, adaptation to a faster change rate will not be possible. The sequences of conferences that were planned were expected to take a year and in the event were spread over eighteen months. Their effects within this space of time (which are fully reported in the book) were very considerable. This is to be regarded as an important finding.

Central to the method chosen was the decision that senior managers on the locations must themselves directly assume leadership of the dissemination process. The continued demonstration and experience of their commitment to the philosophy would provide the most essential precondition for its acceptance by the rank and file.

Later, many members of middle management could also assume leadership roles and from the learning they gained by so doing a critical mass of capability could be built up for the implementation phase. Implementation could not be delayed until the dissemination process was completed as far too much expectation had been created. Accordingly, a third top management conference was convened in March 1966 to decide on the implementation strategies. Working out these constituted the third research task.

The main recent experience of Tavistock in this field had been in setting up pilot projects which could act as centres of organisational learning in bringing about socio-technical change. These had been particularly successful in the Norwegian industrial democracy project on which the Institute was simultaneously engaged in conjunction with the Institute of Work Psychology in Oslo. Accordingly three pilot projects were set up in one of the large refineries but they did not go well. They were too slow and too open to disruption by day to day pressures and from changes in key personnel. Moreover, the degree of concentration on them drained off resources from other possibilities. This was resented. The pilot projects were to some extent in contradiction to the spirit of the whole undertaking which had aimed to include everyone.

The massive nature and speed of the dissemination process, however, gave the possibility of an alternative strategy—namely, the use of departmental managers across the company as the principal change agents. This was directly in keeping with the philosophy. A number of these managers were enthusiastic. What they needed was an instrument which would enable them to proceed independently in effecting socio-technical change in areas of their choice. Accordingly two analytical models were developed—one for production units and one for service units, and short training courses in their use arranged. These could not have been constructed apart from the experience gained in the pilot projects, so that in the end the indirect contribution of these was considerable and led to an innovation much needed in socio-technical studies.

The second main strategy of implementation which emerged was again a direct result of the dissemination process. This involved the other main area of the company development programme—that concerned with productivity bargaining. With the widespread inclusion of shop stewards and trade union officials in the conferences and as a result of their largely favourable response, it became possible to set up joint working parties with representatives of the company to explore key issues before they came to the bargaining table. These working parties were able to use the data collected by the study teams set up at the beginning of the company development programme, so that there was a unique opportunity for informed discussion to take place. Though the various working parties fared unevenly, they put forward a number of recommendations of a far more advanced character than would normally have been expected. The extent of their contribution was not recognised until the bargaining process itself got under way. They formed a new type of "temporary system" and they exercised far-reaching influence as a "reference group" even when they were no longer meeting. They may be regarded as a major innovation in the conduct of industrial relations.

Still another strategy which emerged was use of the philosophy and of socio-technical concepts in the design process for new plants. A major opportunity to do this arose from the fact that a new refinery was under construction and would in due course be brought on stream. The social system judged most appropriate to the very advanced technology of this refinery was assiduously worked out by the staff appointed in terms of the new concepts, with not a few repercussions on the technological choices made. A major effort was also made to select and train the supervisors and workers who were to be employed. Such opportunities are rare. They merit full and systematic study. The new concepts were also used in bringing into being new plant in existing refineries, significant contributions being made by some of the workers.

With the dissemination process drawing to a conclusion and implementation activities well under way the next step was to attempt an evaluation of progress. This led to the fourth critical top management event. Rather than hold a conference which would be central, even if off-site, the managing director decided that it would be more appropriate for this new purpose to hold two on-site conferences, one at each of the major locations. The general managers of each location were to attend both conferences together with the key headquarters people. The conferences were scheduled for April 1967. The fourth research task consisted of working out methods which would enable an assessment to be made.

Though the social sciences abound in techniques of appraisal and follow-up most of those available are suitable only for small-scale discrete problems or else are restricted to survey methodology which has only limited suitability for monitoring the dynamics of change processes. Innovation therefore was called for in any case but improvisation also became necessary, as there was some urgency on the part of management to have a review made. A considerable investment had been made in the project not only in money but in the time spent by a very large number of company people. One had to ask not only what were the costs but what were the opportunity costs of the high degree of preoccupation with the project especially on the part of senior management.

The best chance of obtaining relevant results, it was thought, would follow from the selection of broad areas of change likely to reflect the influence of the philosophy. Four areas were selected: organisational change and job-redesign to represent the effects of the dissemination process; increased personal commitment and pursuit of company objectives to represent the effects on individuals of what they had experienced. Any gross change in the volume or the direction of effects in these areas against a level which might be established to represent the norm of previous years would give a first indication of the strength of the impact which had been made.

Unfortunately, it was not possible in the time available to construct and test a reliable questionnaire or to conduct interviews in depth with the set of key informants chosen (the departmental managers) in a way which would have yielded properly codable and quantifiable results. A wealth of qualitative material was obtained which served the immediate operational purpose but which contained little which could be treated quantitatively. Enough experience was gained, however, to show that such material could be gathered in the future. It would involve a substantial undertaking. Nevertheless, the feedback which becomes available from a systematic evaluation of performance is essential if processes of organisational learning are to be maintained with the consequent gain in adaptive capability. As big an effort must be made about evaluation as about any other aspect of such work.

After the two assessment conferences a number of changes took place, described in some detail in the main text, which lowered the level of activity associated with the project. This was a disappointment to those most intimately involved, but it may in the longer run prove to have been beneficial if renewal of activity at a higher level subsequently takes place in forms appropriate to the changed circumstances. For the pace of the first two years was hot. This was necessary in order to develop the momentum which made it possible to get to first base, but such a pace may not have been sustainable, apart altogether from the dispersion of key people and the interference of external events. We know very little as yet about how to steer change processes of the depth and scope of the Shell philosophy project—except that the basic timescale is a very long one, the vicissitudes many, and that some of the most promising growths get arrested or simply attenuated.

A very important new development has been the production of this book. It will objectify the project outside Shell. There are many people in the management world, the trade union world and the academic world who need to know about it and in whom it will arouse intense interest.

For me personally it has been a deeply satisfying experience to have Paul Hill here at the research centre with which I am now associated during the days when he has been completing the final revision of his manuscript, to go over with him the main happenings and meanings of a project with which I have remained closely identified even after I was no longer actively involved, and to write this concluding note from the Tavistock viewpoint.

Eric Trist

Management and Behavioral Science Center
Wharton School
University of Pennsylvania

APPENDICES

Appendix 1

Craft Unions Involved
in the Negotiation of Agreements
with Shell UK Limited in the early 1960s

Ardrossan   The Amalgamated Engineering Union

Stanlow   The Amalgamated Engineering Union
The Amalgamated Society of Woodworkers
The Amalgamated Union of Building Trade Workers
The Constructional Engineering Union
The Electrical Trades Union
The National Amalgamated Society of Operative House and Ship Painters and Decorators
The National Union of Sheet Metal Workers and Braziers
The Plumbing Trades Union
The United Society of Boilermakers and Iron and Steel Shipbuilders and Structural Workers

Shell Haven   As for Stanlow, plus:
The Heating and Domestic Engineers' Union

Note: Some of these unions have since further amalgamated

Appendix 2

Some Hypotheses
about the ways in which tasks may be
more effectively put together to make jobs

1   Optimum variety of tasks within the job. Too much variety can be inefficient for training and production as well as frustrating for the worker. However, too little can be conducive to boredom or fatigue. The optimum level would be that which allows the operator to take a rest from a high level of attention or effort or a demanding activity while working at another and, conversely, allows him to stretch himself and his capacities after a period of routine activity.

2   A meaningful pattern of tasks that gives to each job a semblance of a single overall task. The tasks should be such that although involving different levels of attention, degrees of effort or kinds of skill, they are interdependent. That is, carrying out one task makes it easier to get on with the next or gives a better end result to the overall task. Given such a pattern, the worker can help to find a method of working suitable to his requirements and can more easily relate his job to that of others.

3   Optimum length of work cycle. Too short a cycle means too much finishing and starting; too long a cycle makes it difficult to build up a rhythm of work.

4   Some scope for setting standards of quantity and quality of production and a suitable feedback of knowledge of results. Minimum standards generally have to be set by management to determine whether a worker is sufficiently trained, skilled or careful to hold the job. Workers are more likely to accept responsibility for higher standards if they have some freedom in setting them and are more likely to learn from the job if there is feedback. They can neither effectively set standards nor learn if there is not a quick enough feedback of knowledge of results.

5 The inclusion in the job of some of the auxiliary and preparatory tasks. The worker cannot and will not accept responsibility for matters outside his control. Insofar as the preceding criteria are met then the inclusion of such "boundary tasks" will extend the scope of the worker's responsibility for and involvement in the job.

6 The inclusion in the job of tasks requiring some degree of care, skill, knowledge or effort that is worthy of respect in the community.

7 The job should make some perceivable contribution to the utility of the product for the consumer.

8 Providing for interlocking tasks, job rotation or physical proximity where there is a necessary interdependence of jobs. At a minimum this helps to sustain communication and to create mutual understanding between workers whose tasks are interdependent, and thus lessens friction, recrimination and "scape-goating." At best this procedure will help to create work groups that enforce standards of co-operation and mutual help.

9 Providing for interlocking tasks, job rotation or physical proximity where the individual jobs entail a relatively high degree of stress. Stress can arise from apparently simple things such as physical activity, concentration, noise and isolation if these persist for long periods. Left to their own devices, people will become habituated but the effects of the stress will tend to be reflected in more mistakes, accidents and the like. Communications with others in a similar plight tends to lessen the strain.

10 Providing for interlocking tasks, job rotation or physical proximity where the individual jobs do not make an obvious perceivable contribution to the utility of the end product.

11 Where a number of jobs are linked together by interlocking tasks or job rotation they should as a group:

(*a*) Have some semblance of an overall task which makes a contribution to the utility of the product
(*b*) Have some scope for setting standards and receiving knowledge of results
(*c*) Have some control over the "boundary tasks"

12 Providing for channels of communication so that the minimum requirements of the workers can be fed into the design of new jobs at an early stage.

*13   Providing for channels of promotion to foreman rank which are
sanctioned by the workers.*

The above hypotheses are merely intended as an illustration of the sorts
of matters we would wish to keep in mind in studying the chosen factors.

F E Emery
Tavistock Institute of Human Relations

Appendix 3

Commentary on
Statement of Objectives and Philosophy

1 PRIMARY OBJECTIVE

Objective. The primary objective should not be seen as a finite target or goal which can be achieved and then superseded by some other target, but rather as something which the company continually seeks to achieve. This requires continuous adaptation to changes in the environment and a continuous attempt to improve upon current performance. The primary objective has three elements:

1   The first paragraph expresses the company's basic economic objective; as an economic enterprise the company must strive to continue to exist and to grow
2   The second paragraph expresses what might be called the company's social objective; as a member of society the company must contribute to the growth and development of society.
3   The third paragraph defines the company's Group environment

The first two elements must be considered together since they are inter-dependent. The role of the company in society is seen to be the creation of new wealth (element 1) and the meeting of society's requirements for products and services (element 2).

The conflict which is sometimes seen between elements 1 and 2 is resolved in as much as the company commits itself to maximising its contribution to Group profitability only through the more efficient conversion of social resources into products and services: thus, at the same time, society is better served and contribution to Group profitability is enhanced.

Profitability. This is the new wealth or the difference in value between the input of total resources and the output of products and services. It should not be confused with "distributed profits" which is simply that portion of the total profitability which is distributed to shareholders.

Insofar as this arises from increased efficiency. The company commits itself to seeking profitability only through increased efficiency. It rejects the alternative of appropriating wealth through exploitation of any of its resources.

Legal rights of privileged access. The company has privileged access to those resources in respect of which it has concluded agreements or contracts; e.g. land leases, contracts of employment, etc. The company, however, does not own these resources in any absolute sense; they remain part of the total pool of resources of society. The major implication is that the company remains accountable to society for the proper and efficient use of these resources.

The commitment to protect and develop society's resources applies only to those resources which the company makes use of and must be interpreted in accordance with prevailing standards and values of society.

Ultimate discretion. This paragraph makes it clear that ultimate discretion—that is, responsibility for taking decisions—for maximising Group profitability, must rest with the Group, the only level at which a full picture of all relevant factors is available. It follows, therefore, that the company cannot operate as if it were an independent enterprise and as if its primary objective were simply to maximise its own profitability.

There will be occasions when in the interests of overall Group profitability, the company may be required to operate suboptimally. The word "ultimate" implies, however, that the company can contribute to Group's decision taking by feeding-up information and advice. This point is developed further in specific objective 3 in section 2.

2   SPECIFIC OBJECTIVES

This section sets out six specific objectives to be pursued at company level. In the process of implementation of the philosophy it will be necessary to translate these specific objectives into a hierarchy of subsidiary or dependent objectives to be pursued at refinery, department and section levels.

Specific objectives 1 and 2. These two represent the key objectives which derive from the primary objective. All the other specific objectives contribute towards their fulfilment. They express the fundamental dilemma of the management position in that in all decision making there is the continuing need to balance current profitability against making provision for future profitability.

"Optimal." There is the need to make the best choice between present and possible future requirements which may well be conflicting.

"Minimum expenditure of total resources." This is not to be interpreted as minimum financial cost; it is concerned with the minimum expenditure of total resources "appropriate to the discharge of its (the company's) responsibilities to the group" (c.f. primary objective). It would clearly be inappropriate to restrict either volume or quality of production simply in order to reduce financial costs.

"Decreasing." The objective for the future must be to increase efficiency, i.e. to reduce costs per unit of quantity and quality.

"Decreasing" (specific objective 2) identifies the future trend line;

"Minimum" (specific objective 1) is concerned with the actual situation at any particular point in time.

It is to be noted that the pursuit of these objectives will require the development of yardsticks or standards of performance to enable managers to assess accurately their achievements in relation to them, or dependent objectives derived from them.

Specific objective 3. This specific objective derives from the last part of the primary objective. It has two main implications:

1   There is a need for a continuous creative two-way flow of information and advice between the centre and the company. This is necessary to ensure that the company fully understands group's policies and appreciates the implications of Group's requirements; conversely, it is necessary that Group be made aware of all relevant knowledge that might affect its decisions on matters relating to the company's activities (e.g. the feed-back of operational know-how for the benefit of design teams in BIPM). The company has the right and the responsibility to challenge Group decisions where they do not appear to be making the best use of the company's capabilities.

2   Where the company carries responsibilities it is necessary that com-

mensurate power should be available to the company to make its decisions effective in the fulfilment of its responsibilities. "Power" in this context means:

(*a*) Authority to expend various resources of the Group in carrying out assigned responsibilities; and

(*b*) The competence or capabilities of its staff in the sense of skills, knowledge, intelligence, etc.

Specific objective 4. The implications of this objective are developed more fully in section 6 which is concerned with the way in which conditions may be created appropriate to the development of individual potential.

The commitment is limited by the phrase: *"In contributing towards the company's objectives."*

The primary objective must remain the key criterion so that the development and realisation of the potentialities of people cannot be encouraged or brought about to such an extent that the overall use of resources is made less efficient; e.g. it would not contribute towards the company's objectives to assist an employee in learning to play a musical instrument, although he may have potential in that direction.

Specific objective 5. It is recognised that all industrial activity interferes to some extent with some amenities of the community, although, perhaps, improving or creating other amenities at the same time. This specific objective commits the company to seeking to reduce the interference caused by its activities, and indeed commits the company to some measure of leadership in this respect ("accepting the measures practised under comparable conditions in British industry as a minimum standard . . ."). The extent to which the company would go beyond this minimum standard in any particular case must remain a question of managerial judgement and will be influenced by the environment at each location.

3   THE PRINCIPLE OF
JOINT OPTIMISATION AS A GUIDE TO IMPLEMENTATION

Any production system is made up of two elements:

A social system: made up of people, with their particular physical and psychological requirements and characteristics and their organisation, both formal and informal in the work situation.

A technical system: comprising the equipment and plant, with its particular characteristics and requirements and the way it is laid out. In the general development of thinking about work organisations, two main schools of thought have been identified:

1 One which looks at work organisation largely in terms of the technical system, and which has been called the scientific management school. The approach is basically mechanistic, efforts being concentrated on perfecting the technical system and man being regarded simply as an extrapolation of the machine. This has led, for example, to such features as division of productive tasks into their basic elements, precise definition of jobs, minimising skill at the shop-floor level and the setting-up of detailed systems of external control and supervision.

2 The other, which has been called the human relations school, looks at work organisations largely in terms of a social system. It concerns itself largely with the physical and psychological needs of the worker, in general, without particular relation to the technology or the actual tasks to be carried out. Thus, attention is concentrated on physical environment, general working conditions, welfare items, management/worker relations.

The work of Tavistock and others over the past decade or so has led to the development of the view that a work organisation must be regarded not as a technical nor as a social system, but as a joint socio-technical system, and that the type of interrelationship between these two subsidiary systems is crucial to the effectiveness of the organisation. To achieve the best performance from the organisation as a whole it is necessary to design the social system jointly with the particular technology. This entails defining the nature or the fundamental characteristics of the technical system and translating it into jobs or tasks which take account of the essential needs and characteristics of human beings. (c.f. section 6 where these are discussed).

The relationship between men and machines is seen as essentially complementary; men with their flexibility and powers of discretion are good at doing those things which machines are not good at doing, while machines with their consistency and predictability are good at doing the things that men are not good at doing. Thus to optimise the operations of the organisation as a whole it is necessary to design men's jobs so that they are related in a complementary way to the technical system.

One implication of this concept is that to achieve the best overall results it may be necessary to place certain limits on what is attempted, either in the social or the technical system. On the other hand, it means that where there is a proper matching of mutually supporting and complementary systems, the overall result is better than the sum of the two parts if maximised separately.

This section occupies a key link role in the structure of the statement. The company is accepting the principle of joint-optimisation as a guide to the pursuit of its objectives; this expression of the principle leads on to an analysis of the interrelationship between the technical and social systems (sections 4, 5 and 6). It thus establishes the relevance of the remainder of the statement to the achievement of the objectives set out in the earlier sections.

4 KEY CHARACTERISTICS OF THE EVOLVING TECHNICAL SYSTEM

This section defines seven technical characteristics which are considered to be fundamental to the nature of the company's activities and to its environment, now and in the foreseeable future. These must form the starting point for any attempt to achieve the most appropriate match between the technical and the social systems.

Key characteristic 2
Wide measure of flexibility. . . . It has been noted that this characteristic is less valid for chemical operations, where the degree of flexibility is considerably less than in oil refining activities.

Added value. . . . Value added to crude oil and intermediate oil products in converting them into finished products. This value is, of course, only realisable in the market.

Given and variable inputs. Because of the company's situation in an international Group manufacturing function, refinery feedstocks are largely allocated to the company by Group and are made up of a wide range of different crude and intermediate oils.

Key characteristic 3
Measures of efficiency and plant utilisation. Two measures:
(*a*) Level of plant utilisation
(*b*) The costs involved in achieving that level

Plant reliability. This depends upon three main factors:
(*a*) Plant design, level of spares, etc
(*b*) Method of plant operation
(*c*) Plant maintenance

5 IMPLICATIONS FOR THE SOCIAL SYSTEM

This section identifies the major implications for the social system of the fundamental technical characteristics identified in the previous section. Despite the complications arising as a result of the diversity of activities and technologies within the company, the most significant consequence is shown to be that the effective operation of the system is critically dependent upon the processing of information by people within the social system and, arising from this, the need for employees at all levels to be committed to their task and to exercise a high level of personal responsibility.

The rapid and increasing rate of change. . . . The general argument of this paragraph is that where there is a rapid rate of technical change, it is only possible to make the most effective use of this change in the overall system by planning the joint development of both the social and the technical systems.

Commit it to train people in new skills and new knowledge. . . . A particular consequence of rapid change is that skills and knowledge more rapidly become obsolete. Where such obsolescence results from the company's or the industry's technical developments, the company has a special responsibility to re-equip its employees to enable them to fulfil a useful role in society, either within or outside the company. Where, however, obsolescence occurs as part of the general development of society, responsibility for retraining and redeployment of individuals is shared by the company with the community in general.

The most significant consequence of characteristics 2, 3, 4, 6 and 7. . . . Throughout the company, at all levels and throughout all functions, employees are involved in either obtaining, or contributing in some way to the processing of, information that is ultimately to be used for the control of the technical system. In this context the "processing of information" includes, for example, such activities as the actual recording and analysis of technical data and the formulation of administrative policies. In the majority of instances, the processing of information in this way will involve contacts between people; the resulting network of contacts, or relationships, forms a social system through which information flows. The conditions appropriate to the effective functioning of people in such a social system are quite different from those sufficient for the effective functioning of machines in a purely technical system. Some of the appropriate conditions, relating to the work situation, are set out in section 6.

And to a large degree in the exercise of craft skills. . . . Although craftsmen are required to exercise some physical effort in their work it is considered that their most significant contribution is in the form of technical knowledge or information. The strength expended in the turning of a spanner is less important, that is, than that the spanner should be placed on the right nut.

The only promising way of avoiding these faults. . . . The only promising way of avoiding these faults that has so far been identified by social research in this field is that described in the statement. It is possible, of course, that there are other promising methods that have not yet been identified or expressed in the literature on the subject.

Internally motivated. . . . The statement is concerned here, of course, with positive "internal motivation." It is, perhaps, possible to generate negative internal motivation through such external stimuli as threats of physical punishment or fines, etc. The latter interpretation would clearly be inconsistent with this general context and with the statement as a whole.

A more common term for an internally motivated person is perhaps a "self-starter," a man who exercises self-control and self-regulation, who initiates action and requires little supervision.

External control. External to the individual, mainly through supervision.

6 RESPONSIBILITY AND COMMITMENT

This section is concerned with the creation of conditions in which positive internal motivation may develop. The company recognises that it cannot simply expect commitment from its employees, still less can it demand commitment from them. It can do not more than set out to create the conditions under which such commitment may develop. This involves emphasis upon psychological requirements rather than upon the material terms and conditions of service. It is essential to have satisfactory terms and conditions of service if there is not to be continual friction over them, but their existence is not in itself sufficient for the development of positive commitment.

This list is not intended in any way to be exhaustive but is considered to embrace the major psychological requirements. It is the result of work carried out at different times in a wide range of industries and in a number of different countries.

Requirement 1
The work must not be too demanding of the employee nor must there be too much variety, either in the elements of a particular job or in the number of positions which an employee may be required to fill in a given period of time. Either of these conditions could be inefficient, leading to reduced effort on the part of the employee, as a result of his frustration or alienation. On the other hand, too little variety or insufficiently demanding work would also lead to inefficiency through boredom, or fatigue arising from it. The optimum level of variety in any particular job will differ with the nature of the tasks involved and the environment in which they are carried out; in general, however, there should be some variety in the pace and demands of a job so that, for example, a man is enabled to take a rest from a high level of attention or effort or demanding activity, while working at another task, or conversely, is enabled to extend himself after a period of relatively routine activity.

Requirement 2
This requires that there should be some effective means of recording or noting a man's performance, and examining its implications with him.

Requirement 3
This requires:
  (a) That a man must have some measure of freedom in the way he carries out his work
  (b) That he should not be severely penalised for certain types of mistakes; the occurrence of mistakes should lead not only to

rectifying action, but also to their analysis as part of the learning process

(c) The provision of some measures or yardsticks by which the employees' growth may be identified

Requirement 4

This implies some degree of formalisation in the definition of areas of discretion. An employee needs to know what are the prescribed limits within which he may exercise his discretion. The exercise of discretion is seen as the most distinctive human capability. Where a man is not enabled to exercise discretion in some way, he is being used in a sub-optimal way; the job needs redesigning or it needs to be mechanised.

Requirement 5

"Social support." There is a need for jobs to be designed in such a way that they provide some opportunity for a man to have some contact with, and the support or assistance of others in carrying out his work. This need can often be met, for example, through the formation of work groups or teams. This does not necessarily mean that men have to work in close proximity to their fellows (e.g. craftsmen in pairs) provided that when working in physical isolation, there is some provision for support of this kind.

"Recognition." There is a need for a rational system of recognition, as expressed, for example, through the distribution of status and the various forms of reward, and related to the differing levels of contribution to the company's activities. Persistent irrationalities in the distribution of recognition are likely to cause dissatisfaction and alienation.

Requirement 6

The job should include some element of care, skill, knowledge or effect that is worthy of respect within the community.

Additionally, an employee is more likely to be able to commit himself to the objectives of the company if they can be seen to fulfil some worthwhile purpose in society. There is little difficulty about the company being able to fulfil this particular requirement since petroleum products play so prominent and vital a part in the life of the community.

Requirement 7

What is considered to constitute a "desirable future" will vary widely between individuals. Examples of what might be considered as desirable are: the opportunity to plan ahead afforded by security of employment and stability of earnings; opportunities for promotion; opportunities for increase of skill and knowledge; increase in responsibility or simply continued employment in a job which exercises an individual's responsibilities.

"They cannot generally be met, however, simply by redesigning individual jobs. . . ." The psychological requirements listed exist for the individual in the work situation. This paragraph is concerned with the fact that in attempting to meet these needs through the redesign of jobs it is essential to bear in mind the interrelations between different jobs and between groups of jobs. We are concerned, that is, not only with the redesign of individual jobs but with overall organisational development.

"Responsibilities should be defined in terms of objectives to be pursued." In the process of implementation of the philosophy, it is essential that jobs at the different levels and throughout the functions have their objectives defined, deriving from the specific objectives.

"Although procedural rules are necessary for co-ordination. . . .' Procedures, rules and regulations are necessary for the effective co-ordination of the diverse activities in a complex organisation; but mere compliance with them should never come to replace the pursuit of objectives. Such procedures must remain subsidiary and need to be continually reviewed and changed in keeping with the changing requirements.

"The company must seek to ensure that the distribution of the various forms of reward is consistent with the levels of responsibilities carried by the individual." It is considered essential that the system of reward be based upon rational criteria and be consistent with the responsibilities carried by individuals at different levels throughout the organisation, the responsibilities carried being considered the main criterion upon which to judge the individual's contribution to the company's activities.

Appendix 4

Simplified version of the Statement of Objectives and Philosophy

1   OVERALL OBJECTIVE

This expresses the company's main purpose in life. It has two parts.

The company is one of a large group of companies known as the Royal Dutch/Shell Group. One main part of the company's purpose in life (like any other subsidiary company) is therefore to contribute as much as it can to the overall growth and profitability of that Group. It cannot pursue its own profit as if it were independent.

Secondly, in trying to contribute as much as it can to the Group's profitability, the company commits itself also to certain obligations to the society in which it operates. It does this by recognising that all the resources it uses (land, material, men, etc) are in the last analysis still part of the total pool of resources of society: i.e. the national economy. By accepting this belief the company openly undertakes the obligation to use and manage all its resources in such a way that they are protected and developed: i.e. not misused or degraded.

The company combines these two parts into a single overall objective. It commits itself to making its contribution to Group profitability and to the national economy by pursuing at all times the most efficient use of the resources available to it. How the company intends to do this is discussed at greater length later on.

One further point about profitability; it is not used here to mean that percentage—a relatively small percentage—that is paid out by Group to the shareholders. It means the total amount that is earned on the operations of the Group companies and that is paid out in a very wide variety of ways: for example, wages and salaries for employees, taxes to governments, research to find more efficient methods and better products, and stable prices for customers.

2 SPECIFIC OBJECTIVES

The overall objective which has just been defined above, is concerned with the wider role the company plays as a member of the group and as a member of the total society in the UK. This section converts the overall objective into six precise objectives for the company to aim at in carrying out its major activity, namely manufacturing petroleum products:

(a) The company has to meet orders made for petroleum products. It must attempt at all times to meet these orders with the most efficient use of its resources; men at all levels, materials, finances and equipment.

(b) At the same time the company must also plan for the future, so that it will be in a position to meet future orders in the most efficient way. It will need the appropriate equipment, of the right capacity, and men with the right skills and knowledge to operate and maintain it. Without such planning the company cannot remain competitive.

(c) As a member of the Group, the company has to fit into the group picture. The whole of this picture can be seen at Group level; the company can see only a small part of it. Thus, for example, certain crudes may be sent to the refineries and certain products may be demanded, that seem to be inefficient and even unprofitable in the smaller refinery picture; whereas in the larger Group picture they are both reasonable and profitable.

On the other hand the refineries have better knowledge of the performance of the plant and equipment they operate. They can, in many cases, help Group to make better decisions on the use of this plant and equipment. Thus the company has a responsibility to pass this knowledge upwards and to question higher level decisions when it believes it right to do so.

(d) A vital area is the use made of the men we employ—our human resources. To allow men at all levels to make their greatest contribution, we must be concerned with the way they are managed, the way their jobs are made up, the way they are trained and the way they are allowed to feed in their own ideas about their work.

(e) All operations must be managed and carried out with the highest regard for safety.

(f) The company must remain comparable with the best companies in the UK in trying to control and reduce inconvenience to the communities in which it works, caused by fumes, oil leaks, etc.

3   JOINT OPTIMISATION

In its objectives the company is committed to the most efficient use of its resources. This section explains the means the company intends to use in pursuing increased efficiency.

It will do this by applying the principle of joint optimisation of its technical system on the one hand, and its organisation of people on the other. What does this mean?

The word "optimum" means "the best" as distinct from "the maximum." Optimum, therefore, always implies a balance. The best meal is not necessarily the biggest meal. The "optimum" output at which to run a plant or a machine is not necessarily its maximum output, for to do this might result in a short life between repairs, high maintenance costs and an overall loss of output through shutdowns. The "optimum" output in this case would be that which gave the best balance between production and maintenance and hence in the long run the lowest costs (and also, over say a year, a higher output, owing to the saving in shutdown time).

So in our case "joint optimisation" means that all problems at all levels in the company, whether they concern the design of plant, staffing, work practices or anything else will be tackled in the light of both the technological and the human needs: the best results will be achieved by a balanced solution to both needs. We do not want excellent tools in the hands of uninterested men or good men having to work with poor tools.

In short the technological and human systems of the company have to be developed hand in hand. In practice, this means that it is not sufficient simply to design a plant to be technically efficient and then to put in a group of people to operate it. Similarly, it is not sufficient simply to establish good human relations between managers and supervisors and between supervisors and men without paying attention to the sort of work they are required to do and the way their jobs are made up.

Neither of these approaches is sufficient because neither looks at the whole picture. To achieve and maintain a better overall performance the company must take into account both technical factors and human abilities and requirements in designing and managing its operations.

There is nothing starry-eyed about this; the value of this principle of joint optimisation has emerged quite strongly from studies in industrial organisations and in operational research during the last decade.

4 HOW JOINT OPTIMISATION CAN BE APPLIED

In this section we begin to examine what it means in practice to apply the principle of joint optimisation in the company. We do this by describing the main technical characteristics which we think will still be with us over the next five to ten years, and by spelling out the implications they have for the people in the company and the way they are organised.

Key technical characteristics and some of their implications
(a) The refining of petroleum products is part of a complex industry that depends very largely on science for its technology. (It is, as they say, a science-based industry.) It is in a constant state of change owing to the rapid advances in scientific knowledge, and the speed of this change is accelerating. As a result the patterns of work and the specific skills required of the people operating refineries are subject to increasing change.
(b) Refining is also what is called "capital-intensive." That simply means that there is a very large amount of money invested in plant, equipment, buildings and so forth in relation to the number of people employed. It is true that there are some activities—handling and packaging for instance—in which a relatively large number of people are employed in relation to the amount of money invested in the plant and equipment. This does not, however, change the overall pattern, which is capital-intensive.
(c) Since, in a capital-intensive industry, the major part of the manufacturing cost of its products is the cost of plant, it is obvious that the most important factor in keeping the cost low is the efficiency with which this plant is used. One way of getting efficient use of plant is automation. This is essentially a matter of detecting any variation from the proper conditions and automatically correcting it, or compensating for it by altering conditions somewhere else along the line. It is used, as you know, to some extent already in our refineries and will be used even more in future as new processes are developed. Instrumentation is also vital to efficient plant utilisation. By providing the operators with detailed information about what is going on inside the columns and vessels, etc, it enables them to make appropriate decisions, or even,

when necessary, decisions that override the automated controls. Even with sophisticated automated controls, there are inevitably occasions when human intervention can lead to better results; provided, of course, that the operators of the plant have got their wits about them, know their stuff and make responsible decisions.

Another obvious and important factor in securing efficient use of the plant is the skill and knowledge of the maintenance engineers and craftsmen. In other words a capital-intensive company like ours is in the final analysis highly dependent on people using their skill and knowledge in a responsible way.

(d) This is all the more important because of the great flexibility that exists in the major refinery processes. The value that can be added to crude oil by processing it depends very much on the skill with which this flexibility is made use of by everyone involved to meet the varying demand for different products.

(e) Finally, one has to take account of the fact that a refinery is very large and the people are dispersed over a wide area. The problems of communications are therefore very much more difficult than those of most factories with their closely-knit groups of people doing similar or interrelated work. It means, in fact, that effective communications have to be carefully built into the system—the informal and sometimes almost unconscious communications that might well serve a small and closely knit work place are certainly not good enough under our conditions.

5 MATCHING THE
SOCIAL (OR HUMAN) STRUCTURE TO THE TECHNICAL ONE

By the social structure, we do not, of course, mean the off-duty social life of a refinery—clubs, amateur theatricals, and that sort of thing. What we mean is the whole complex business of how people interact with one another; how they feel towards their jobs, and whether they are interested or bored by them; how information passes from the man who has it to the man who can use it; how much responsibility people have and how they know they have it.

The social structure in this sense can take a wide range of different forms. There are several choices open to the company. It is important, however, that the social structure be made to match as closely as possible the technical characteristics listed. Two things are immediately clear. First, as we have said, the efficiency of a refinery is, and will continue to be, heavily dependent on the people manning it. Second, the old-fashioned idea that you could drive people to work hard and well by standing over them would (even if it were true) not generally work in our industry. We depend upon people being able to make some decisions themselves, and to accept responsibility for making them well.

People cannot be expected to act in this way, unless they are, in psychological terms, internally motivated: this means interested in, and committed to their work. It means too, that they must feel that the company's objectives are worthwhile, and the sort of objectives they are willing to commit themselves to. What can be done to help people feel this way about their jobs?

6 COMMITMENT TO WORK

Clearly the company cannot just sit back and expect men to develop this sort of commitment and interest themselves, nor can this simply be demanded. What management can do, however, is to set out to create the right sort of conditions under which it is hoped men at all levels will develop interest in and commitment to their work.

The company believes that there are two essential elements for creating such conditions; neither one on its own is sufficient:

(i) Good terms of service, including wages and salaries, which are fair within the company and comparable with other companies of the same calibre.

(ii) A continuing concern for man's fundamental psychological needs in relation to his work.

What are these needs? A lot of work has been done on this and the main ones have been identified as follows:

(a) The need for some element of challenge and variety in the work

(b) The need for some area in the job, however small, which a man can call his own and in which he can take his own decisions

(c) The need for some form of feed-back to let the man know how he is getting on in the job

(d) The need for learning so that a man at least has a chance to keep his skills up to date and possibly increase them

(e) The need for work to be organised and planned in such a way that a man gets the support and assistance of his colleagues when he needs it

(f) The need to know something about the way in which his particular job fits into the overall department or company picture

Q

(*g*) The need for a man to feel some element of hope about the future. This can take many forms—such as, security of employment, stable income, maintenance of skills, possible increases in resibility, possible promotion, etc

Not everybody experiences these needs. Not everybody experiences them to the same extent or with the same degree of emphasis. It is believed, however, that most men do experience them and that unless the job allows men to fulfil at least some of them, their work becomes frustrating and boring. Clearly such a state of affairs is not only very inefficient for the company, but it is unsatisfactory for the man himself; a very large slice of his life becomes a burden, to be tolerated only as a means of earning a living.

The company believes it must take these needs into account in the way it makes up individual jobs, and also in the way it organises jobs together in groups and departments; people must know what their job is, what its main objectives are, how it is related to other jobs and what sort of decisions they are permitted to take.

But it goes further than this. Refinery design, for instance, cannot be done in purely technological terms; it must include human capabilities. Or to put it another way, we must recognise in our design thinking, that people have a specific contribution to make in the eventual operation of the plant. This is simply being realistic. People are a factor in the situation, whether we take account of them or not. If we do not take account of them, with their needs and capabilities, we will not achieve the best design.

There are two more very important points.

The company must ensure that responsibility and authority are bracketed together, so that men have the authority to carry out the job they have been given to do.

Secondly, the company must plan to build up a wage and salary system that fairly rewards the different levels of responsibility that men carry and the different levels of contribution they make to the company's effort.

6   PUTTING THIS PHILOSOPHY INTO PRACTICE

This philosophy is new. In fact the formal decision to run a company on these lines is, so far as we know, unique in this country. However, it is one thing to say one is going to do something and quite another to do it. One thing that makes it so difficult to put this kind of thinking into practice is that verbal or written communication is not enough. Not nearly enough. This is a written communication. We have done our best to put over clearly what we are trying to do and why. But is it now clear to you? Do you believe that anything worthwhile will come out of this? Have you any idea of what it will mean to you in your job? We think it would be difficult for anyone to give a straight "yes" to the questions even after a close study of the document.

How then can this philosophy be made a living reality instead of a mere statement of intent?

First, it will inevitably be a slow process; it is not something that can be imposed by management from above. It would not work if it were because such imposition is dead against the spirit of the thing. In fact, because it is a philosophy—a way of thinking about the company's function as an industrial organisation in society—and not a bill of rights, no one knows in detail what its implications are at all levels. So, putting it into practice must inevitably be a process of growth. Of course problems will arise and these must be met and overcome as they arise.

The senior managers of all the fineries have worked through the major implications of this philosophy. They are committed to it. It is the managers' job now to involve people at all levels in working out how it can make their jobs more productive and satisfying. The degree of success achieved in carrying this out will depend directly upon the energy and tenacity that is put into it.

One final comment: This is a business-like philosophy. Its object is to make the company more productive. But it accepts the fact that it can only do this really successfully if everybody at all levels wants the same. So in helping to make your own job more to your liking you should also be making the company more productive. And it is on a continuously improving productivity that the security of your own future can be assured.

Method of Socio-technical Analysis

STEP 1 : INITIAL SCANNING

The objectives of this step are to identify broadly the main characteristics of the production system and of the environment in which it exists and to determine, if possible, where the main problems lie and where the main emphasis of the analysis needs to be placed.

It is envisaged that this will be done through a briefing of the action group by the departmental manager or by someone deputed by him at one or more discussion sessions.

The briefing needs to be fairly carefully structured and should cover the following ground:

1 The general geographical layout of the production system
2 The existing organisational structure and the main groupings within it
3 The main inputs into the system—with specifications where appropriate
4 The main outputs from the system—again with specifications where appropriate
5 The main transforming processes that take place within the system
6 The main types of variance in the production system and their source, for example, the main variances might arise from the nature of raw material or the nature of the equipment, or breakdowns, etc
7 The main characteristics of the relationship between the production system and the department/refinery in which it exists
8 The objectives of the system, both production and social

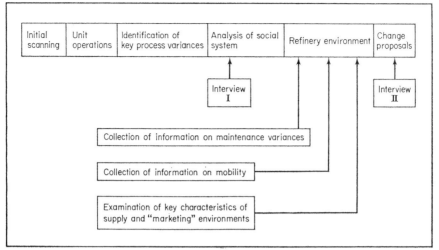

FIGURE A5:1   METHOD OF ANALYSIS FOR SOCIO-TECHNICAL SYSTEMS
Approximate order of analytical steps

STEP 2 :   IDENTIFICATION OF UNIT OPERATIONS

The purpose of this step is to identify the main phases in the production operation. Unit operations are here taken to be the main segments or phases in the series of operations which have to be carried out to convert the materials at the input end of the system into the products at the output end. Each unit operation is relatively self contained and each effects an identifiable transformation in the raw material; a transformation in this sense being either a change of state in the raw material, or a change of location or storage of the material.

The actions necessary to effect the transformation may be carried out by machines or by men but we are not at this stage concerned with either the characteristics or needs of the machines (e.g. maintenance needs, operating characteristics, etc) or the characteristics and needs of the men (e.g. psychological needs). The focus of attention is entirely on the series of transformations through which the raw material goes.

Where possible the purpose of each unit operation needs to be identified in terms of: its inputs, its transformations and its outputs.

STEP 3 :   IDENTIFICATION OF KEY
PROCESS VARIANCES AND THEIR INTERRELATIONSHIP

The objectives of this step are to identify the key process variances and the interrelationship between them.

By variance we mean deviation from some standard or from some specification. It is necessary to emphasise two points:

1   At this stage in the analysis we are concerned with variance that arises from the raw material or from the nature of the process itself as it is currently or normally operating. We are not concerned with variance that arises from faults in the technical equipment or plant (e.g. breakdown or malfunctioning) nor are we concerned with variance that arises from the social system (e.g. mal-operation or human error).

2   We are not concerned with the total range of variance. From studies of this type that have been carried out it has been found that in any production system there are a large number of variances that have either no effect or a comparatively minor effect on the ability of the production system to pursue its objectives. We are not concerned with variance of this order at this stage in the analysis, although it may be necessary to take some such variance into account in subsequence attempts to reach a higher level of joint optimisation. At this stage we are concerned only with those variances which significantly affect the capability of the production system to pursue its objectives in one or more of its unit operations. We have called these variances "key variances" and propose certain criteria for their identification (see (c) 2 below). The sequence of actions necessary to carry out this stage of the analysis is as follows:

(a) Identification of all variances in the system (arising from the nature of the raw material or from the nature of the process) which, in the opinion of the action group it is considered worth while to take note of.
The main source of information will be the manager and supervisors of the system, drawing upon their knowledge and experience.

   From experience gained in similar studies it will be necessary to work over this list of variances several times to ensure that all the main variances are included.

(b) Drawing up a matrix of variances.
Taking the variances identified in (a) above, drawing up a matrix, the main purpose of which is to help show up any localised clusters of variances—control problems. It will also begin to show where information loops exist or are necessary in the production system.

In addition it will also help in the selection of key variances (e.g. variances that have an effect through a series of unit operations are likely to be considered key to the control of the process).

(c) The identification of the key variances:
We propose that this be done in two stages:

1   The department or unit manager and his appropriate assistants should make out a list of what they consider to be the key variances—drawing upon their experience and knowledge of the production system

2   The action group should work over this list, checking it against the matrix of variances and against the following four criteria. A variance should be considered "key" if it significantly affects any one of these
  (i) Quantity of production
  (ii) Quality of production
  (iii) Operating costs (use of utilities, raw material, overtime, etc)
  (iv) Social costs (e.g. the stress, effort or hazard imposed on the men)

The first three dimensions are concerned with the system's production objectives. The last one is concerned with the production system's social objectives, that derive from the social objectives written into the company's statement of objectives and philosophy. With the identification of these key variances it is possible to move into an analysis of the social system, to examine the way in which it contributes to their control, and so to the attainment of the production system's objectives, and also to examine the extent to which the social system's own needs are met.

STEP 4 : ANALYSIS OF THE SOCIAL SYSTEM

The objective of this step is to identify the main characteristics of the existing social system. It is not intended, however, to map or describe it in all its aspects, with all its complex sets of interrelations and groupings, both formal and informal. It is hoped that by structuring the analysis carefully it will be possible for the analytical team—the action group—to draw out relatively quickly, sufficient of the relevant information to enable it to begin to develop job-design proposals. The following steps are, we consider the minimum necessary:

1   Brief review of the organisational structure where necessary, filling in a little more detail than was included in step 1 on number of levels, social groupings and types of roles.

2   Table of variance control (Figure A5:2).
This is a key step in the analysis of the social system, in terms of control of variance. Its purpose is to show the extent to which key variances are at present controlled by the social system and it has been found possible

| KEY PROCESS VARIANCE | NAME OF UNIT OPERATION | | | BY WHOM? (ROLE NOT PERSON) | CONTROL ACTIVITIES | BRIEF DESCRIPTION OF INFORMATION RELATED TO THOSE ACTIVITIES AND SOURCE | HYPOTHESIS FOR JOB DESIGN |
	WHERE OCCURS	WHERE OBSERVED	WHERE CONTROLLED				

FIGURE A5:2 METHOD OF ANALYSIS FOR SOCIO-TECHNICAL SYSTEMS
Table of variance control

by its use to identify where key organisational and informational loops exist or are required. It answers the following questions:

(a) Where in the process does the variance occur?
(b) Where is it observed?
(c) Where is it controlled?
(d) By whom?
(e) What tasks does he have to do to control it?
(f) What information does he get and from what source to enable him to carry out these control activities?

An additional column has been added to the table, headed "Hypotheses," because it has been found that in using the table suggestions or hypotheses for change tend to arise and it is considered worth while to note these at this stage for subsequent discussion and possible validation.

3 Ancillary activities. Filling out the descriptions of the workers' roles in the production system. In the variance control table mentioned above activities connected with the control of key variances will be listed. It is likely, however, that there will be a number of ancillary activities. Identifying these and trying to relate them to the control of the process may well lead, for example, to the identification of other forces operating in the social system, or the identification of additional key variances. On the other hand it could conceivably lead to the questioning of these ancillary activities altogether.

4 Spatial and temporal relationships. Mapping out the physical or geographical relationship between the various roles in the production system (e.g. distances, or physical barriers betwwen workers) and their relationship over time (e.g. over shifts or over a normal working day).

5 Flexibility. Using a mobility chart (Figure A5:3) it is possible to identify the extent to which the workers in the production system share a knowledge of each other's roles. It may be necessary to carry out this step in two phases; an initial analysis, simply identifying where workers rotate, and a more detailed phase, where this appears appropriate, examining the extent to which they carry out the essential tasks associated with the roles.

To be properly representative the mobility chart should cover an adequate period, say two or three months. It is therefore considered appropriate to set up the recording of this information in the early weeks of the process of analysis.

6 Payment system. Setting out the pay relationship between various

SHIFT NUMBER. . . . .

NAME	CATEGORY	Day 1			Day 2			Day 3			Day 4		(etc)
		M	A	N	M	A	N	M	A	N	M	A	N

FIGURE A5:3 MOBILITY CHART

1 To be completed by the chargehand or foreman as appropriate

2 To be completed each shift for a period of, say, two months

3 In the shift columns shown above, the job carried out by the man during that shift to be entered (each of the available jobs could be numbered or given a letter to make entries easier)

roles in the production system. This will have its impact of course upon job rotation, group working, etc.

7 Psychological needs. Testing out the roles against the list of psychological needs. It is considered that a simple adequate/inadequate rating against the main activities is sufficient. For this purpose the action group will need to rely on the manager's and his supervisor's or chargehand's perception of the roles. For the workers' perception of their roles it will be necessary to set up some machinery for the collection of their views. (c.f. step 5).

8 Mal-operation. Identification of areas of frequent mal-operation and establishment, where possible, of causes.

STEP 5 : MEN'S PERCEPTION OF THEIR ROLES

This step is also part of the analysis of the social system. It is dealt with separately, partly because of its importance and partly because of the method of carrying it out. Its purpose is to learn as much as possible of the men's perception of their roles. We are specifically concerned with the extent to which they see them fulfilling the psychological requirements. It is considered that this should be accomplished perhaps by a personnel man attached to the action group, either as a full member or for this particular purpose.

It is proposed that he should run interviews with appropriate groups of men on two occasions; one within the first six weeks say of the analysis beginning, and the second towards the end of the process when job-design proposals are being finalised. Both interviews will be highly structured, designed by the action group with open-ended questions based on the general area of the psychological requirements, and in the case of the latter interview, on the developing job-design proposals.

With this step the analysis of the production system itself is complete, and it is certainly to be expected that a number of redesign proposals or hypotheses will have emerged by this stage.

The analysis now goes on to consider the impact upon the production system of a number of "external" systems—for example, maintenance, supply and user systems, refinery personnel policy, etc. These stages will influence any hypotheses that have emerged and may well throw up further redesign proposals.

STEP 6 : MAINTENANCE SYSTEM

This step is not concerned with the examination of the maintenance system or organisation as such. It is concerned solely with the extent to which that system impacts upon the particular production system which is being analysed. Its particular purpose is to identify the extent to which the maintenance system affects the capability of the production system to achieve its objectives. Thus the objectives of this step may be stated as follows:

1   To determine the nature of the maintenance variance arising in the production system
2   To determine the extent to which that variance is controlled
3   To determine the extent to which maintenance tasks should be taken into account in the design of operating roles

This does not mean, of course, that this analysis of maintenance variance is in any way subordinated to the analysis of process variance carried out in step 3. Both are necessary to an understanding of the characteristics of the production system.

It may be in some cases that variance of a greater order arises from the maintenance system than from the production system itself, in which case one would expect greater emphasis upon this particular stage.

For the purpose of this stage we propose the collection of information on maintenance activities in the form set out in Figures A5:4 and A5:5, beginning within the first month of the project and being continued for say two or three months. We consider that the collection of additional data and the burden of collection placed on operating and maintenance staff should be kept to the minimum consistent with achieving the objectives of the analysis, and the attached pro-formas are therefore as simple as possible. They are, of course, in common with the rest of the method, open to development and improvement.

STEP 7 :   SUPPLY AND USER SYSTEMS

Once again this step is not concerned with identifying the characteristics of the supply and user systems in themselves. The focus of the analysis is on the way in which these environmental systems affect the particular production system that is the focus of the project. The objectives are:

1   To identify the variances that are passed into the production system but that arise in the system which supplies the raw materials, or the system which dispatches and (where appropriate) uses the products of the production system

| MAINTENANCE ITEM | ORDERED BY (JOB NOT NAME) AND DATE ORDERED | LOCATION (UNIT OP) | COMPLEXITY | | DATE FINISHED | CRITICALITY IN RELATION TO OBJECTIVES | | | |
			NO. OF CRAFTSMEN	TRADES INVOLVED		QUANTITY	QUALITY	UNIT COSTS	SOCIAL COSTS

FIGURE A5:4 MAINTENANCE ACTIVITY—EXCLUDING SHUTDOWN MAINTENANCE

1 To be completed by e.g. process chargehand, process foreman, maintenance foreman

2 To be completed each shift for a period of 2–3 months

MAINTENANACE ITEM	DEPARTMENT MANAGER	TECHNICIAN	SUPERVISOR	CHARGEHAND	TOTALS	
					YES	NO

FIGURE A5:5   MAINTENANCE ACTIVITY—EXCLUDING SHUTDOWN MAINTENANCE

1 The list of maintenance items to be drawn from the survey of maintenance activity indicated in Figure A5:4
2 Each of the people shown in the columns to indicate by marking "yes" or "no" whether in his experience operators in the process could, with a reasonable amount of training, carry out this maintenance item

2   To examine, where this seems appropriate, the extent to which these variances could be controlled closer to their source, or their effect upon the production system diminished

In general it is considered that the analysis across the boundaries of the production system should be kept to a fairly general level initially, and only continued in greater detail where there appears a real possibility of effecting an improvement, e.g. a better control of variance or more appropriate flow of information.

The result of this step might either be a diminishing of the variance arising in the production system from across its boundaries, or, in some cases, a redefining of the production system's objectives to ensure that they take realistically into account both supply and "marketing" constraints.

STEP 8 :   REFINERY ENVIRONMENT AND DEVELOPMENT PLANS

The purpose of this step is to identify those forces operating in the wider departmental or refinery environment that either affect the production system's ability to achieve its objectives, or are likely to lead to a change in those objectives, in the foreseeable future. It has two main sub-steps:

1   Development plans. The identification of any plans, either for the short or medium term or those long-term plans which have a high probability of being implemented, for the development of the social or the technical systems. These clearly would have to be taken into account in the development of any redesign proposals

2   General policies. The identification of any general refinery policies or practices which impinge upon the production system, where these have not already been taken into account in the examination of the maintenance system and the supply/user systems. Examples of these might be the general method of promotion, which affects the social system, or the utilities supply and control system operating throughout the refinery, which affects the technical system

Once again it should be emphasised that we are not concerned with an examination of the characteristics of these environmental systems as they exist in themselves, but only insofar as they affect the ability of the production system to pursue its objectives. In the analysis of most production systems these environmental factors will constitute "givens" rather than areas to be included in proposals for change.

STEP 9 : PROPOSALS FOR CHANGE

The purpose of this step is to gather together all the hypotheses and proposals that have developed during the process of analysis, to consider their viability and to present them with sufficient structure to form the basis of a subsequent action programme.

As has been mentioned above, it is likely that hypotheses will begin to arise as the analysis of the technical system is being completed. It is likely that these proposals will be added to, eliminated or modified as further information is gathered about the social system and about the environmental systems.

Those hypotheses that remain at the end of the process of analysis have to be tested, as far as is possible on a theoretical basis, against appropriate criteria before being developed into viable proposals. The actual mix of criteria will vary from project to project and will require careful design. These criteria must, however, relate to the production systems objectives—they must cover, that is:

1   The production objectives of the system—concerned with production in terms of quantity, quality and general operating costs. This covers proposals specifically aimed at increasing the control over or diminishing variance in the production system

2   The social objectives of the production system. This covers proposals aimed at, for example, increasing the extent to which psychological needs are met in role design and those aimed at diminishing the costs borne by the men in the social system, (e.g. stress, hazard or heavy labour)

Many proposals will, of course, lie in both areas, e.g. proposals aimed at increasing the level of responsibility in the lower levels would both meet the psychological requirements and perhaps lead to shorter lines of communication and more effective variance control. In addition, any proposals for the redesign of the social system must be tested out against emergency and crisis needs. In the case of a process unit for example this would entail the ability to shut the unit down in the event of loss of power or feed, or major fire.

R

Appendix 6

Method of Role Analysis

INTRODUCTION

This has been developed in conjunction with the method of socio-technical analysis as an alternative method of analysis for departments where no continuous process exists, such as service or advisory departments. As in socio-technical analysis, its purpose is to help managers to analyse their existing organisations, as they currently and normally operate, and to produce proposals for change where this seems likely to lead to improved performance. It is very much in the development stage and it is hoped that it will be improved by experience of practical applications.

There are seven steps:

STEP 1 : GENERAL SCANNING

This should provide a general introduction to the outputs, inputs and transformation processes in the department, that is its objectives, its work and its organisational structure and location within the overall organisation, as well as the geographical layout of the department. This scanning is necessary so that the more detailed investigations of these areas, which will follow later, can be seen against an overall background. One problem here is to decide upon the amount of detail at this level: in general this should be kept small. It is probably useful for the departmental manager, supposing this analysis is being undertaken by an action group, to describe what is going on rather than to explain its purpose, leaving the other members of the group to ask for reasons if they wish.

STEP 2 : THE OBJECTIVES OF THE SYSTEM

It is important, if possible, to arrive at a clear definition of objectives, since this provides a rational datum against which to judge all activities in the department. In practice the identification and statement of objectives pose difficulties since, for example:

1   The objectives stated may be so general as hardly to be a guide to action
2   They may be multiple, but only one or two may be identified
3   They may be non-measurable
4   They may refer to several time periods, c.f. philosophy statement, specific objectives, 1 and 2
5   They may be partly derived from a higher or other system level
6   They may be outputs which the system wants to minimise rather than to maximise, e.g. waste
7   They may involve changes of the internal structure of the system rather than outputs from the system (i.e. change in assets)
8   They may not yet be well enough recognised to be formulated

In order to cope with these problems the following method of analysis is proposed:

To consider firstly all major outputs of the department whether they are processed raw materials, communications, men, or anything else. Secondly, to try to identify all inputs. Thirdly, to follow through these inputs and determine the steps by which they are processed before they become outputs; to make sure in fact that no significant output has been missed. These outputs are then tested to determine whether they are objectives by presenting them to the manager of the next higher system level, and asking him whether or not these are the outputs required. However, these are not the only input transformations: it is clear that a department is not only utilising its inputs in order to process them and transform them into required outputs, but some inputs are coming into the department in order to maintain or develop the assets, and part of the objectives of a department will be directed towards these two activities. The assets of a department should be taken to include its plant and equipment, the money over which the manager may have authority, and the men.

In considering a department's outputs, a problem may arise in that it may not be possible to describe an output such as a communication (written or verbal) meaningfully unless some indication is given of its necessary contribution to an overall decision being made outside the boundaries of the department. In such cases it is useful to draw up a table with the following headings:

1   Description of output
2   To whom sent
3   To what overall decision was it intended to contribute
4   What was the required contribution of the department's output to this overall decision

—and a final column indicating the consequences of sub-standard performance in respect of the social and economic cost, both inside and outside the department. The above analysis will determine the resources which are within the boundaries of the department, and those the manager needs to call upon. The departmental objectives should now be clearer and against this background it should be possible to begin to hypothesise the:

1   Responsibilities
2   Authorities
3   Information/communication links with others
4   Key methods and procedures

—which are appropriate, and to match these against those which exist and are identified particularly in steps 3 and 4.

STEP 3 : ANALYSIS OF THE ROLES IN THE SYSTEM

An analysis of each role in the system in the same way used in step 2 in order to arrive at the role objectives, relating them back to the overall departmental objectives. This process should start at the top with the manager's role and work downwards.

STEP 4 : MEASUREMENT OF ROLES AGAINST PSYCHOLOGICAL REQUIREMENTS

Having identified the inputs, transformations and outputs of each role, it is then useful to measure:

1   The manager's perception

2   The man's own perception of how far each role meets the psychological requirements as set out in the philosophy. The men's perception of their own roles can be achieved by individual interviews to be carried out preferably by someone outside the department

STEP 5 :   GROUPING OF ROLES

The analysis will identify the necessary role interaction links insofar as the current process exists and will lead to hypotheses about the clustering of these roles in respect of their geographical and temporal distribution and status dimensions.

STEP 6 :   DEVELOPMENT OF CHANGE PROPOSALS

It can be expected that in the course of the preceding steps various hypotheses for change will have emerged. These should now be refined into proposals for the redesign of jobs or organisation—for example, a change in authorities or methods of grouping; or it may be that analysis by this stage will have indicated a need for a reformulation of departmental objectives. Proposals for change will of course have to be related to the wider environment of which a department is a part.

STEP 7 :   MANAGEMENT BY OBJECTIVES

Once the objectives of the department and its constituent roles have been determined, attention should be given to developing measurements of performance; the setting of targets (either jointly agreed with a manager or for self-monitoring), and how these results might be fed back to the man occupying the role (so that a man should know not only "what his job is (but) how he is performing in it" . . . philosophy statement).

Bibliography

BLAKE, R R and MOUTON, J S, *The Managerial Grid,* Gulf, 1964

BROWN, W, *Exploration in Management,* Heinemann Educational Books, 1960

EMERY, F E and OESER, O A, *Information, Decision and Action,* Cambridge University Press, 1958

EMERY, F E and TRIST, E L, "The Causal Texture of Organisational Environments," *Human Relations* 18.1, 1965

EMERY, F E and THORSRUD, E, *Form and Content in Industrial Democracy,* Tavistock Publications, 1969 (Norwegian edition: Oslo University Press, 1964).

FLANDERS, A, *The Fawley Productivity Agreements,* Faber and Faber, 1964

FORD, R N, *Motivation through the Work itself,* American Management Association, 1969

HERZBERG, F, MAUSNER, B and SNYDERMAN, B, *The Motivation to Work,* Wiley, 1959

HIGGIN, G and JESSOP, N, *Communications in the Building Industry,* Tavistock Publications, 1966

HUMBLE, J W, *Improving Business Results,* McGraw-Hill, 1968

JAQUES, E, *The Changing Culture of a Factory,* Tavistock Publications, 1951

KAHN, H and WEINER, A J, *The Year 2000*, Macmillan, 1967

LEWIN, K, *Field Theory in Social Science*, Tavistock Publications, 1952

LIPPITT, G L, *Organisation Renewal*, Appleton, Century, Croft, 1969

MANN, F, *Studying and Creating Change: A Means to Understanding Social Organisation*, Industrial Relations Research Association Publication number 17, 1957

MASLOW, A H, *Motivation and Personality*, Harper, 1954

MCGREGOR, D, *The Human Side of Enterprise*, McGraw-Hill, 1960

NORTH, D T B and BUCKINGHAM, G L, *Productivity Agreements and Wage Systems*, Gower Press, 1969

PAUL, W J and ROBERTSON, K B, *Job Enrichment and Employee Motivation*, Gower Press, 1970

RICE, A K, *Productivity and Social Organisation: The Ahmedabad Experiment*, Tavistock Publications, 1958

ROETHLISBERGER, F J and DICKSON, W J, *Management and the Worker*, Harvard University Press, 1939

SADLER, P and BARRY, B. *Organisational Development*, Longmans Green, 1970

SCHEIN, E, *Organisational Psychology*, Prentice-Hall, 1965

TAYLOR, F W, *The Principles and Methods of Scientific Management*, Harper, 1911

TRIST, E L and BAMFORTH, K W, "Some Social and Psychological Consequences of the Longwall Method of Coal-getting," *Human Relations* 4.3, 1951

TRIST, E L, HIGGIN, G W, MURRAY, H and POLLOCK, A B, *Organisational Choice*, Tavistock Publications, 1963

VAN BEINUM, H, *The Morale of Dublin Busmen*, Tavistock Publications, 1966

Index